The Every Person's Guide to Accelerating Careers in Big Multinational Companies

A Blueprint for Building High Impact Careers and High Performance Organisations

KEN J. LEE

PARTRIDGE

ISBN: Hardcover 978-1-5437-6871-8
Softcover 978-1-5437-6873-2
eBook 978-1-5437-6872-5

Print information available on the last page.

To order additional copies of this book, contact
Toll Free +65 3165 7531 (Singapore)
Toll Free +60 3 3099 4412 (Malaysia)
orders.singapore@partridgepublishing.com

www.partridgepublishing.com/singapore

CONTENTS

To Crystal
With love, for always pushing me to be my better self.
KL

To Amar
My heartfelt appreciation for your wisdom and friendship.
KL

Acknowledgements

This book is dedicated to the extraordinary teams and managers I have had the privilege of leading and working alongside and for throughout my twenty-five-year working career. Many of the career and project stories that appear in this book are yours. Everything I have learnt, as Sir Isaac Newton puts it, has been through standing on your collective shoulders.

To my wife of fifteen years, Crystal, thank you for always pushing and supporting me to be better, including writing my first book at the ripe old age of forty-six. While it has led to some heated debates, without you, I would have avoided many precious experiences in my life by being on the safe road. I would probably still be eating burgers and playing video games.

I dedicate this to my friend, mentor, guru, and former manager, Amar, the wisest man I know, for uncannily knowing when to reach out your hand to pull me off the ground no matter where you are in the world and for showing me the light in many a dark tunnel.

I dedicate this to my grandfather, Toong Lin, for setting the bar so high on being a good human that I will need my whole life to get there and never have want for something to aspire to.

Lastly, I dedicate this to my buddy, Michael, who taught me the meaning of friendship and unconditional support.

Preface

I am currently transitioning to an exciting new role in a new company. While this is not unfamiliar territory for me career wise, this transition has been particularly difficult. I worked nine years, had an incredible run at my previous company, and completely underestimated the amount of emotions and fear of change pulling out those roots would bring. As I navigated this new challenge, I had the chance to have long overdue chats with many people whom I have interacted with, mentored, or coached over the years. Because of these unexpected challenges, I received words of advice and encouragement from this group of people. The thing that struck me about this experience was how strange it was to have my own advice given back to me as well as how consistent and repetitive it was. I interpreted this surprise to mean these words of advice were meaningful and effective throughout time, with different personalities and across organisations. Given the value both I and this group of people had derived from these lessons, I felt an urgent need to put the thoughts down formally in writing both to allow more to benefit and as a reaffirmation/stocktake of my values and team management strategies as I start this new journey.

Another inspiration for the work to follow has come from my experience as I prepare for my new job. I took the opportunity to review a number of books that have been on my to-read list but just never made it because of the hustle and bustle of the day-to-day. What I noticed was an abundance of literature around entrepreneurship, transformation, innovation, and other big ideas – very entertaining reading and certainly relevant to those at a C-suite or higher level of management. However, I found these challenging to implement for those starting out in their careers or taking on their first few leadership positions or the underdog just trying to be better.

I also found that most of the literature did not cover specifically the group of organisations that do the lion's share of employment: large multinational organisations (MNCs). To manage the expectations of the scope of this initiative, this is focused on building impactful careers in large MNCs that typically operate almost like big biological organisms. While I believe some of the insights will be useful, they are not specifically for entrepreneurs or those working for start-ups or early-stage companies where there is already a good amount of literature providing insights on this scenario.

The other reason for my focusing on MNCs, to be upfront, is that this is where I have worked my entire career. MNCs are heavily criticised in my industry as being dinosaurs on the verge of extinction. While some good arguments support this prediction, it is a criticism I largely disagree with. MNCs do a tremendous amount of good, although as with all things, there are pros and cons. They first employ a lot of people and provide these employees and their respective families a livelihood – no small matter. Many of them also perform important corporate social responsibility work, supporting important charities and the like around the world. In addition, they have the ability to scale and invest in important ideas, enabling them to reach the masses and change the world. A great example in my line of work is the tremendous efforts to find vaccines and treatments for the COVID-19 pandemic. Given the importance and the wealth of resources within MNCs in the world, any effort to help their teams be more effective would not be wasted. This piece of work aims to help the 'cells' – the managers and employees – of this organism of an MNC proactively build accelerated and impactful careers and, in so doing, create more value for these organisations that enables them, in turn, to do more good things for the world in the area that they operate in through a win-win scenario. I also have perhaps somewhat of a childish vision that if we can create such a culture for a win-win scenario where scores of crack teams throughout a large MNC are not only doing their day-to-day work but also finding special projects to work on that will improve the company, its customer experience, and its products, this would be an amazing place to work and one that will sustainably help make the world a better place.

I write this from two vantage points – the new, young employee and the new manager – because in big MNCs, the first lesson to learn is that you can't work alone. In addition, it is this group that is often missed out in the literature as their plight is less sexy than that of those directly at the forefront of changing the world. Teamwork is essential, and this foundational pairing is one of the most effective units, in my opinion. I toyed with how to write on these two vantage points but, in the end, chose to put them side by side so the reader can understand both perspectives, calling out, where appropriate, each side's specific viewpoint. I have also used very broad terms around value creation and making the world a better place because while I have worked mostly in healthcare, I do feel these basic ideas are applicable to a broader field of disciplines.

The examples and stories contained here have all come from amazing managers/bosses who have led me over the years, my personal experiences, and those I have had the good fortune to lead, although I have blinded them to protect the 'innocent'. The stories come in two angles, first on the projects themselves and then about the careers of individuals affected by the projects in discussion. I have tried my best to acknowledge them as well as acknowledge the work of others which they may have referred to in their lessons to me. However, this acknowledgement may be incomplete, and I apologise in advance for this and invite feedback so I can do what is necessary in upcoming versions. I also can't claim too much as my own work or ideas but instead state my role merely as a scribe and organiser of this collective wisdom. To ensure personal privacy in the various stories, I have used aliases to make the text easier to read and generalised some of the examples where needed. Where things could be more safely specific, I have left them so. As individuals and projects have been used on more than one occasion, the consistency of aliases and descriptions will also make them easier to follow.

I will start with the foundation of building an accelerated career with impact in an MNC: the special project. It is not easy to be recognised by senior leadership while working on our usual day job. While important, the day job is also more predictable, expected, and arguably lower in terms of overall impact within the larger sphere of a big MNC. One has to step out of one's job description (JD) to find a project that is strategically important or unusual to the organisation to allow visibility to be created in addition to generating exponential value for the organisation beyond the day job. An important caveat here – I am certainly not saying you should abandon your day job to play politics – is that to build an accelerated career with impact, you just have to do this on top of the day-to-day. In addition to its visibility, the conduct of a special project will enable the building of a broader network in the organisation as well as lessons critical to accelerating careers.

I will discuss which projects to consider and, where none exist, how to create one. Special projects are, by nature, highly ambiguous and difficult to work on. Knowing this, I wanted to share some stories and experiences to help you start and work through road blocks that will inevitably come up and finally, upon completion, effectively communicate the outcome and, for want of a better word, claim credit for your efforts. This is because ultimately, there is no point in creating something of potential value but never letting it be unleashed.

Although the focus of this book is on accelerating careers through the special project, you will find many stories and examples that illustrate lessons which are useful in the business as usual within an MNC. Do consider the thoughts in the 'How?' and 'So Now What?' chapters as potential concepts that can be expanded more broadly in building an impactful career.

In the words of one of my favourite Marvel Cinematic Universe (MCU) heroes, Carol Danvers, 'higher, further, faster, baby'. Onward and upward.

Ken Lee
Singapore

Why the Special Project?

Having witnessed multiple accelerated careers over time, I have found each case to often consist of a few critical ingredients:

1. Extended **visibility** in the organisation
2. Creation of a **good reputation**
3. Organisational **networks**
4. Diverse **experience** beyond the day to day
5. Accelerated and relevant **learning**

Of all the tools available to use in accelerating one's career, the special project is one of the rare few that often fulfils this full house of critical ingredients. In start-ups and smaller organisations, day-to-day projects often have all the qualities of a special project – highly strategic, highly impactful, and highly visible to decision makers. As such, you don't need a special project to stand out from the crowd. You also don't need one to get a diverse range of experience because one typically does a lot more of the scope of a given project in a start-up versus an MNC, where there is a lot of specialisation and teams to throw at it. However, when you are working in a larger MNC, the sheer volume of ongoing business-as-usual projects makes it difficult to see where everything fits and, therefore, even harder to be visible to the leadership of the organisation who make career decisions and allocate resources. Hence, the need to work on a special project that transcends the day-to-day business as usual is highly impactful and unique enough to warrant the high level of visibility and broad learning required.

If performed well, the special project also creates an important partner to visibility: a good reputation. After all, there is not much point being visible for the wrong things! Leading a special project usually means working outside of your usual sphere of people within the day job. Building these types of networks is critical as you ascend to new roles and challenges. These networks may also be decision makers or influencers in your career acceleration. The complexity of a special project will also mean tremendous learning and experience in many dimensions professionally and personally. Such lessons and experiences are unlikely to come by in your day-to-day job but will be so critical for continuing success as you ascend to roles of greater responsibility.

As a manager, your responsibility is to develop your team, enabling them to be better and reach higher than they would have ordinarily without your help. One of the greatest things about MNCs is that there is usually a strong human resources (HR) framework to do this. You can select from a variety of tools to drive the process: training, coaching, mentoring, different jobs, international assignments. Some of the more formal aspects of these tools – such as a business course, like an MBA – certainly have their place in the development of a talent but they are beyond the scope of this piece of work. Having said that, I wanted to highlight key aspects of some of these tools which can be applied and are so useful with a special project in mind. As a manager, you can also play a unique role in finding special projects to work on or create with your employee. This is not to say that the employee is merely a pawn in all this. They should also take ownership of their development, volunteer for special projects that are around, and suggest things to work on. In some cases, for those reading who are employees, you can also take the driver's seat. It really takes a collaborative, open-minded relationship between both the manager and the employee to make things work.

I am a big advocate for special projects versus going outside for development through courses or training or taking on more generic coaching, mentoring exercises. First, if selected well (we will discuss that in the next chapter), it's highly relevant to the organisation. It usually provides experience and learning in a discipline that's important (and relevant) to the organisation. During the course of the project, the manager and the employee will inevitably be coached and mentored by others as well in areas, once again, that are highly relevant. Because of its high relevance and strategic importance, it provides opportunities to be highly visible within the organisation by those who make important hiring and structural moves. We will also discuss how to maximise impact for visibility in the 'So Now What?' chapter. Let's face it – when have we heard the management say, 'Oh, so-and-so completed their MBA. Let's promote them'? Over the years, I have had not only the pleasure but also the huge responsibility of sitting in on numerous talent reviews and restructuring planning where these were discussed. While I am certainly not representative of everything that takes place in MNCs across industries and geographies, let me just say that I have not heard the MBA thing once in over a decade.

'The organisation should plan my career for me.' I often hear from team members and employees that their personal development should be taken care of by the organisation. This is actually a very good point, and it's true; big organisations should do this better. However, big organisations, by their sheer size, just struggle to do this in a disciplined way, which leads us to a situation a little like crying over spilt milk. I like the wisdom around spending time on what you can control (multiple wise sources) rather than on what you can't. It's hard to control the organisation's actions in doing this. Perhaps one day, after multiple successful special projects, you will become the CEO of the company and can actually control this. :-)

For the time being, for the rest of us, we will have to contend with the fact that we cannot control the large MNC we work for. However, we can control our thoughts and actions, and the ideas contained here are largely within our control. Being proactive has been a trait that I have observed on many an occasion which will take people far. So for the employee, take your career into your own hands. Likewise, for managers, in today's war for talent, one has to take an active interest in the careers of one's teams as not everything can be managed at a pure compensation and benefits level. I work in healthcare, an area where the demand for talent dramatically outstrips supply. As managers, we have a responsibility to build talent, regardless of how conducive it is to do so in the organisation that we work for, who can then, in turn, build talent further. A virtuous cycle.

In addition, we have to retain our talent as best as possible. Having reviewed employee retention figures in an effort to improve them for the better part of a decade, I found that the one reason I see people repeatedly cite about why they stay or leave is the presence or lack of career development. The people who have stayed a long time in an organisation typically have had opportunities to work in diverse scenarios that interest them. While those who have left typically went to take on new jobs that offered them the career development that they were seeking. In my humble opinion, this effort to do career development is hugely actionable, which is why it is so sad when it is done inadequately or, worse, not done at all.

A lot of you will want me to speak about money, and I won't run away from it. Yes, compensation is an important factor, no doubt. However, for leaders of large MNCs, all the money in the world is not enough to win the talent war purely on dollars. For sure, we need to pay a healthy market rate, and the one thing with big MNC HR systems is that they know what this is. Market rates are also often computed such that across most grades, they enable an individual to lead a comfortable living for their stage in life. If it is below a comfortable life where an employee cannot pay for their key needs like food, shelter, and family, this, of course, is a problem that no amount of career development can address. Once you take care of the basics, the next step is a little less clear. From my experience, for many, it is purpose, a meaning. For some, it is even more money. For us managers and employers, money will eventually be difficult to address, but we can certainly make an important impact on purpose. A human, at the end of the day, wants to do a good job and know that they are making a difference in the world. For many MNCs, our purpose can indeed do that. When I look at the missions of many MNCs, they are noble ones – a healthier world, a fed world, a safe world, a happier world, or some version of this, not bad things at all. As managers, we need to translate this into what that means for a particular employee's individual situation. We cannot expect the organisation to automatically do it for us, although some may be more helpful than others. That final mile is the skill in management and why you, as a manager, are there.

A reason many people tell me for not wanting to embark on a special project is that 'it's not in my job description'. To be honest, this provokes a big antibody response in me. I find that JDs are like nooses we put our necks in and tighten, so much so that I often fantasise about taking a flame thrower and burning all JDs to the ground. So as not to antagonise my HR colleagues and in all seriousness, I will say that JDs are important at guiding the recruitment process and the day-to-day work – no question about this and their value in these two elements. However, I feel the following statement should appear in all JDs: 'to do *whatever the organisation requires to be successful* as long as it is not ethically wrong or non-compliant to good business practices'. :-) Also, in all seriousness to both our manager and employee readers, one should really look at one's JD as directional in nature and to see beyond it, especially for that career's acceleration. Each one of us has a responsibility to be the best that we can be and not hide behind a piece of paper as a way of justifying why you shouldn't try.

The other 'why I can't' reason I hear a lot is time or the lack of it. 'I'm just too busy and don't have the time.' My response to this is to change your mindset or vantage point in viewing the problem – to see things as solutions rather than problems. For an employee, if your manager is asking you to take on a special project as part of your development, this is not a direct order; it's a discussion. Hence, it means that if time is an issue, then be solution orientated rather than problem orientated. This means to come with a solution for how you can do the special project if time is an issue. You could, for instance, ask to remove some projects from your portfolio or excuse yourself from other activities to create that time, or you could downsize the project or slow down the timeline. Why not ask for these types of solutions rather than having to respond with a flat no? As a manager, be aware also about the practical challenges of issues such as time and be solution orientated to help your employee be able to do this work. Look at it also as setting them up for success as the probability of success is a function of adequate resource allocation. Be open-minded to what can be done to create time. In most cases, while a challenge, time is not an insurmountable one if one is motivated enough.

Having said all this about solutions, which I believe are appropriate, I also wanted to be provocative and say this – there is always gas in the tank, especially for those of us earlier in our careers with less family commitments to attend to. I will raise a concept here of discretionary effort (multiple originating sources) and expand on it in the 'How?' chapter. Essentially, each of us has more time that we can give to an initiative. It's just whether we choose to do so or not. It could be some time over the weekend or one hour added to every day or a shorter lunch. If you are interested in accelerating your career, I will be very direct about this – I'm afraid some elbow grease and good old-fashioned hard work are simply going to be needed.

'It's rewarding.' For a manager, there can be no greater pleasure than seeing an employee develop and rise up to a higher level than what you have even imagined thanks to your intervention. They might even become your boss one day! It's almost like being a parent, seeing them grow. The second more counterintuitive thing for a manager is that your worth is now no longer judged by your direct work output. It's judged by your team's output and how you lead them. While it has not often been said directly to me, too often, junior managers feel threatened when a team member succeeds. However, good organisations and experienced leaders will recognise talent when a manager is able to lead their team to new heights. Conversely, if they see a manager stifling their team members, doing all the work, even if it is of tremendously high quality, this is a negative situation.

An old manager, Ernst, once said to me in my transition to leadership of a bigger team, 'A very capable person can carry a department of ten on their back just through pure physical strength and brute force. But when that team becomes one hundred, they will inevitably collapse under its weight. Poor leadership is not sustainable at critical mass.' I assume that a number of you are reading this because you aspire to lead big organisations and teams. To be able to get there, you need to be able to lead and inspire rather than do the actual work. Another way to look at it is if an employee in the team stars, good assessors also look at the leader. 'Who hired this star? Who created the environment for that star to flourish?' Also, great leaders are never afraid of having their positions threatened because they, by nature, want to vacate them for their next big challenge. It's a virtuous cycle because great employees want to work for such individuals as they are not sitting around, blocking their paths for ascension too. For the employee leading the project, it's also tremendously rewarding. You learn a new skill, engage with new people, and have the satisfaction, hopefully, of delivering outstanding impact from your project. If that should lead to career acceleration, this is another incredibly satisfying outcome. There is just simply tremendous pleasure in winning.

I want, at this juncture, to highlight an individual I know well who represents the sort of career trajectory in leadership of projects that do well, albeit on the more dramatic end. This person, Thena, worked in an entry-level role in North Asia in one of my past organisations. Thena was clearly an individual of considerable talent, studying abroad at Ivy League, speaking multiple languages, and having outstanding interpersonal skills. She was highlighted in a talent review as someone who could be accelerated, and we found her a special project. It was an initiative that was critical to the organisation but required some turnaround because of a number of challenges. Thena took on this initiative even though it meant leaving the comfort of her home country for a potentially risky job that was a contract for only six months. She managed to turn this project around and, because of its strategic nature, had the opportunity to present it to the global head of our department.

Many of the strategies to come were applied in her case. She was subsequently promoted and, over the next five years, rose to the level of director, which was five full grades above her initial starting position, moving to three different countries in the process. Although the trajectory is steep, the thing is Thena is not all that rare in my past experience. While the projects were different, I have seen multiple Thenas in my time and, through writing this book, hope that through a butterfly effect, we can create many, many more. My very own story reads similarly, with three of my biggest promotions being the result of special projects as well. This landmark project that Thena worked on was research on a fairly uncommon form of cancer which, at that time, had very few proven treatment options for it. The results would be referred to even outside of the Asia region where the research was conducted. In fact, it was considered the best research of its kind for two years before being superseded by newer efforts.

'An MNC career can be immensely rewarding.' I recently attended an investment course to become better at assessing businesses, a skill which, in turn, would help me build a better, more sustainable business in my new role. To my surprise, I also had lessons from the participants that were unexpected but nonetheless highly appreciated. Many of the participants were attending because they wanted to be more financially independent so that they could care for their aging parents and reward them for the sacrifices they had made raising the family. They spoke about helping their parents work less in their older age or even retire formally. They spoke about taking the family for a long overdue vacation. To my surprise, I did not hear one thing about Ferraris, jewels or other luxuries! Humans continually surprise me with their capacity for good, and that's another reason why I am trying to write this book.

The other thing that surprised but saddened me was that most of these attendees disliked or even directly hated their jobs. As expected, most of them were working for some form of MNC. While to a certain degree, I can relate to this frustration, I firmly believe this doesn't have to be the case. As managers and employees, we have the ability to make our jobs fascinating and create a passion for leaping out of bed every morning. The other thing for this group is that investment requires capital, and for many of them, it does mean working for a considerably longer time to raise that capital at their hated jobs in MNCs. Why work for decades in this career purgatory? In short, it simply doesn't have to be that way.

One should at least try to take matters into their own hands and make a change. This goes for both the manager and the employee. The special project will help to spark the creativity inside every one of us, and it is also an avenue to try to rectify the frustrations that processes within MNCs create within us. For the individual leading the project, the learning and sense of achievement in completing it are tremendous. However, one should not forget the manager as well. Leading an individual on this journey is not a passive task, and the learning and sense of achievement are just as meaningful for them. We don't have to be victims but rather can transcend this complexity and become that solution. On another note, accelerating your career through special projects will also enable you to rise up that dreaded ladder as well as have larger impacts on the organisation and the world. By definition, this does also translate to higher salaries to accelerate the capital build for investment.

A friend once said that I was making the wrong conclusions here because this investment group was a highly selected population as it was precisely this type of people who would go for such training. I am not so sure this is 100 percent correct, although it does have its merits. I do believe a significant population suffers from this affliction. I am the cofounder of a mentoring group that is trying to grow the Singapore life sciences talent ecosystem. Part of this has involved talking with younger talent in universities and academia as well as those advising them on careers. The data, frankly, from speaking to these individuals who come to this group speak of very similar issues and frustrations. There is an old wisdom imparted to me so many moons ago – I honestly cannot recall its source – that goes along the lines of 'Nothing is ever 100 per cent. We need to act on majorities or significant numbers because inaction is sometimes worse'.

For the managers among you, consider this: a big MNC is basically the sum of many different people and groups of people at the heart. Regardless of what service or product it makes, it's the people that drive it, at least at the present time. I cannot say for sure this will be the case forever as artificial intelligence (AI) continues to evolve, but I dare say some of these lessons may be useful to apply as well for artificial beings, and I look forward to them reading this one day! Having made that somewhat tongue-in-cheek comment, I think it is worth stating that an enormous challenge exists to have the majority of your workforce engaged every day, driving for top performance. A good part of that issue lies with the MNC itself. It develops a lot of processes and red tape to get things done, which unintentionally serves as a disincentive for entrepreneurship and innovation. Perhaps foolishly, I envision a place where everyone can imagine new things, suggest ways to improve the things that we do, and act on them. Imagine a place where nearly everyone is continuously thinking of ways to improve the work that they do, allowed to experiment and then, if successful, implement them. It's hard to imagine this to be the DNA of an unsuccessful organisation. I think a lot of the time, people just get into a rut while working for an MNC because this just cannot occur, and it's just easier to toe the line. However, as managers and employees, we *can* enable it to happen. And isn't that what an MNC is at the end of the day, the sum of many managers and employees.

I have taken a bash here at the complexity and bureaucracy of an MNC. To be balanced, I want to say that this is often necessary and, in fact, has its merits. To get it out there, I do love MNCs, and one can achieve a lot if one can understand and navigate their complexity. Just as an example, some years ago, while working for a big MNC, we were attempting to buy a very interesting small enterprise with a unique capability that we needed. The deal, unfortunately, fell through, and we were beaten by venture capitalists to the goal. During the course of the deal process, the senior executive leading the sell side was highly suspicious. He refused to cooperate with many of our requests in the due diligence assessment of the target company citing us as being too big and clumsy to deal with. In one discussion, we flagged it with the CEO, but he wanted to be hands-off and leave it to his lead. This senior executive was actually promoted to CEO after the deal closure. However, in a turn of events, he was then fired from the organisation in a highly public manner a year later! We subsequently learnt of multiple levels of corruption and non-compliance on his part from the former CEO. The interesting thing is when we heard about the detail of these misdemeanours, we knew they would never have been possible in a big MNC because of the checks and balances we had in place. The same checks and balances that made our due diligence process so 'big and clumsy'.

Managing red tape and complex process reminds me of a phrase I heard once from a professor while at an INSEAD course discussing metrics: 'The path to hell is paved with good intentions'. Like so many words of wisdom that you will see in this book, its origin is somewhat hazy, spoken in some form by intelligent people throughout the ages in many languages. However, like ideas that last for so long, I take them seriously as they probably are on point. Big MNCs have these processes in place to ensure good ethical behaviour, and that is their good intention. However, the path to hell from this is that they become so complex that employees just switch off, blame the organisation, and never think outside the box. This was certainly not the intention, but it ends up being the outcome. MNCs do want employees to rise above their day-to-day, provide inspiration and ideas to improve across the board. Opportunities do exist for this to take place, and my aim in this book is to outline ways to capitalise on this.

I want now to take a more macro, forty-thousand-foot-level view of the why – perhaps a more touchy-feely and philosophical, meaning-of-life view of the problem. As managers and employees, we owe it to ourselves, our teams, and our organisations to discover the very best of ourselves and the reason for why we are here in this world, this planet, this life. It is my firm belief that each of us is not an accident.

One of my favourite movies of all time is *Unbreakable* by M. Night Shyamalan. The story basically tells of a boy who is born with a disease called osteogenesis imperfecta, where his bones are extremely weak and break easily. He naturally has a very difficult childhood growing up, finding his refuge only within comic books. This character, whose name is Mr Glass, wants to know why he exists in the world – 'Do you know what the scariest thing is? To not know your place in this world, to not know why you're here. That's . . . that's just an awful feeling' (https://www.imdb.com/title/tt0217869/characters/nm0000168). I can't agree more and shudder at that thought at times. I think deep down, a lot of us have that fear.

For Mr Glass, one reason for him to exist is if there would be an opposite to him, a super strong person who could do great things for good in the world. So he goes about trying to find this person because it would be validation for why he suffers like he does. The path to this is unfortunately not ideal as he starts committing acts of terrorism in his effort to find his 'Superman', continually looking for a lone person who would be the only survivor in a disaster. He finally finds his Superman, who then, in an ironic twist, is able to bring him to justice. Still, he is so happy for this, stating in the final scenes of the movie, 'Now that we know who you are, I know who I am. I'm not a mistake! It all makes sense!'

Growing up, I was not a particularly ambitious person. I remember at my first job, as a junior doctor in hospital, thinking this was not a bad way to live life, and I had little aspiration to do much more. However, if I asked myself deep down if turning up to work every day sparked some serious passion and meaning, it definitely did not. The word 'zombie', while not quite apt, is in the ballpark of describing this state. Quite by chance, I ended up working within big pharmaceutical MNCs, and that was when I finally felt like I was in the ballpark of developing a passion for work and understanding why I was here. It was incredibly fun to come to work, engaging with global teams all over the world on very diverse projects. At this time, I was just an individual contributor/employee, and to be frank, I once again felt like this was not a bad way to live and became complacent. I owe it to one of my earliest managers, Karl, who continually encouraged me to aspire to be best I could be and showed me how.

In a way, I never wanted to be a manager because guys like Karl were so good at it, and I never thought I would match up. However, as my experience broadened, I realised Karl was actually an outlier, and in fact, I had as good a chance as anyone else at becoming a half-decent manager. An opportunity at that time came for me to leave my home for a job in North Asia. Like Thena's case, it was a business in distress, and the job carried some risk. I took it anyway, taking charge of my first ever team. The rest, as they say, is history. Over the years, I did find my passion: managing and developing people. Many of these stories, you will hear over the course of this book. Healthcare and the concept of making the world healthier are, of course, still passions, but I think of my role now more as managing businesses and teams to achieve that. I, of course, still get giddy with excitement about new science, but my passion, deep down, is developing people and teams to work on the new science. It gets me up to work every day with excitement and passion. Frankly, I can't think of anything else that I would rather do.

Importantly, now that I have seen two sides of the coin – one, doing something just for a job, and the other, working on something I truly believe in and feel passion for – everything is crystal clear. I can understand why Mr Glass felt the way he did. You just can't settle for something to get through life. You need to find or, at the very least, try finding that thing which drives you and brings life meaning, that thing which explains why you are here, and if you have some talent for doing that thing, it is your responsibility to do it to the best of your ability for the benefit of the world. I hope that in pushing for this career acceleration, in working on special projects, many readers will be able to find that reason for being as I have seen happen for myself and others throughout my career.

Stretching outside of that comfort zone into a special project, while carrying some risk, can help us onto a path to discover ourselves. That journey, even if it may not lead to where we expect it to, is worth taking. Arthur, an old manager who will be quoted repeatedly in the coming chapters, said something very profound to me – 'Growth, by its very nature, is painful'. We have to expect that, but it is necessary to becoming stronger and better. Some years ago, in a period of tremendous creativity, I cofounded two start-ups. However, both were in my original yardstick of measurement failures. I remember at that time kicking myself, wishing I had never gone anywhere near this. I had even wished that I had a time machine to go back to change things.

However, when I took more time to reflect, I migrated to a different line of thought. I had learnt so much from those journeys, and more importantly, I challenged myself and failed. I felt proud that I had pushed the limits of my ability. I'm not sure if the words of the great poet Alfred, Lord Tennyson, are appropriate here – ''Tis better to have loved and lost than never to have loved at all'. However, I feel very similar in terms of how these two companies turned out and would never today want to go back to change things. I am happy and proud that I tried and failed rather than not having tried at all. I would still like a time machine though, but it's just to go back and see dinosaurs now.

Which Special Project?

The great thing about MNCs is that there are often special projects in circulation begging for leaders to take them for a run. That is often a great place to start for employees and their managers. Check with the executive team or someone higher in your respective functions from global teams or other regions to see what's on offer. The other benefit of these types of projects is that they are often fairly well resourced and already have a good amount of focus on them.

Having said all this, I want to share a story about the pitfall of a ready-made MNC project for consideration. A mentee once asked me how I selected projects, and instinctively, at that time, I said, 'I look for the one with virtually no one supporting it.' While instinctive, I have found it to be a very useful guiding star. MNCs often have sexy projects that will have double digits (or more) of people working on them. These projects also seem to be on a never-ending quest to absorb even more people into them. I remember reading an interesting article on a business trip flight once talking about various ex-Apple employees who would go on to other successful ventures and what they took from their time at Apple (I am unable to find the reference). I found two lessons of particular interest that still resonate to this day after so many years. The first of these is 'the power of small teams'. This individual spoke about the power of small teams and how these are one of the most effective units, just like the manager–employee partnership. Small teams just get things done more effectively, and there is less ambiguity about who does what. Accountability is super crisp and clear. I am rarely overtly prescriptive in my advice, but this one, I feel so strongly about that I will say it – 'Never pick a project that has an army behind it'. It's so important that I will say it again – 'Never pick a project that has an army behind it'. Just for good measure, *please read the last two sentences again.*

There are also some common scenarios to find special projects. If you have had the chance to be in a merger or acquisition (M&A) situation, there is always a need to integrate the two organisations and find synergies. Invariably, this represents a special project to work on. Many team members often view M&A activity as a terrible situation, especially if you are on the weaker end of a merger or work for the company being acquired. While there is some justification for the concern, one should look at the positives. Many business schools will quote that the Chinese word for 'danger' is similar to that for 'opportunity'. It is a beaten-to-death example but, I do feel, a very useful one to take to heart and practice. Even if you are on the weaker side of the deal, finding critical projects, volunteering for them, and delivering to excellence is a surefire way to secure the next role and possibly one that is even bigger.

New product launches are another area to look into as they typically also require special initiatives to do them well. However, they are often sexy enough to attract too many people for comfort. If that is the case, then look into another segment – the problem projects requiring turnaround. You will see a few of these quoted throughout the book because they are often the ones no one wants. However, the 'danger is opportunity' lesson applies here too. Before I left for my turnaround assignment in North Asia, I have to admit that I felt nervous about it and seriously contemplated not going. My sister said something to me during this time which got me on the plane and that I now recount to many in a similar situation.

She said, 'Brother, it is better to take over a sinking ship than [a] sailing ship.'

That seems rather cryptic, and no, my sister is not a short green creature living in a swamp. When I asked why that was the case, she replied, 'If you take over a sailing ship and it sails even higher, then people will say it was the previous person's work and you are just lucky. If the sailing ship sinks, it is always your fault, regardless of whether it is true or not. If you take on a sinking ship and it truly sinks to the bottom of the ocean, then most people will say that it's not your fault. Poor you for taking over such a basket case as the previous manager botched it up so bad, no one could fix it. And should it sail, then you are a hero, regardless also [of] if you had anything to do with it or not – although one would hope that you did!'

Many big MNCs are continually trying to improve on one thing or another and usually have this basket of special 'transformation' projects in planning to achieve this. These projects usually have things in their names like '2.0', '3.0', 'Next Gen', 'Transformation', 'Bold', 'Big', 'Dream', 'Imagine' – you get the picture. I have found often that because these projects can be quite abstract and complex, there isn't a long line of people looking to participate. Happy hunting!

I'm looking forward to the new Matrix movie, *The Matrix Resurrections*. Their classical metaphor of choosing between the red or blue pill is always a potent reminder to carefully choose your project. I want to go back to that article about the

Apple ex-employees and the key lessons that they took away. The first about the power of small teams, we covered earlier. The second is to 'take as much time discussing the things we don't do as the things that we do'. It really seems counterintuitive to do, but I have found it to be so important in choosing things to do. That individual's point was that whenever Apple had a new release, it was very common for people to say that this or that feature was missing. Actually, it was rare that whatever was called out wasn't discussed, he said. In many instances, they were discussed and thrown out for one reason or another. His point was that every choice has a consequence. Each feature had an impact on weight, size, speed, or something important, and if it was left out, it was deliberate. Spend time looking through the different projects you have found, debate them with your manager or employee, get feedback from outside, and get additional data and whatever else you think you need before deciding which one to choose.

When it comes to running up that list of projects to work on, one useful way I have found and used to help the decision-making framework is the impact difficulty matrix (multiple references, no clear origin, Figure 1). On one axis, try to measure how difficult a project is to do. For example, if it requires a huge budget, requires a large number of stakeholders involved, affects the incentives of people, or violates certain rules of the organisation or industry, this would be classified as difficult. On the other part of the axis, assess how big an impact the successful completion of the project will have on the organisation. Something that markedly improves revenue generation, profitability, the quality of customer engagement, or the quality of delivery would be considered high impact, but first, double-check the 'path to hell' rule. In many of these, the assessment can be quite subjective. You will have to base that on the organisation that you work for and bounce ideas off stakeholders to gauge it better. It doesn't have to be precise, especially if being precise means taking months to come to a decision. Nevertheless, this careful assessment is a critical step to take. Once you have plotted all these on your matrix, you should target the sweet spot of 'easy difficulty, high impact'.

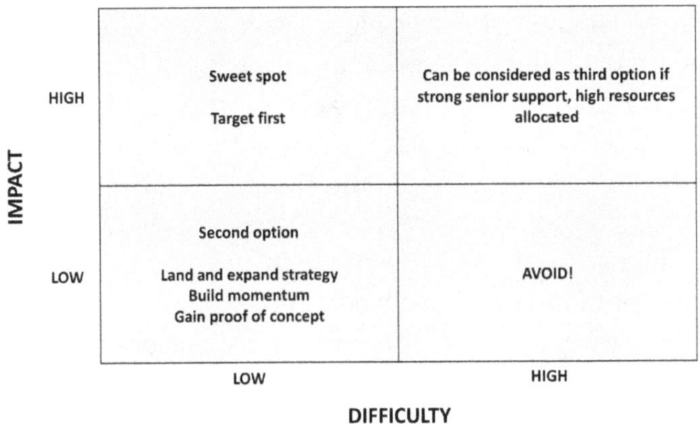

Figure 1: The IMPACT / DIFFICULTY matrix for prioritization of projects for selection

A lot of you will feel that such a project is not readily available because it would already have been thought of. However, I do challenge you to take a closer look. If you are new to the area or team, these projects may be in the trash bin. As unsavoury as it sounds, the project graveyard can be a very rewarding place to look. As an example, I once worked with a department whose goal was to build their scientific credibility to support the claim that their forecasts were of a high quality. This was a critical point for their customers. In their area of business, the ability to publish in significant peer-reviewed scientific journals was seen as one such accepted way to achieve this. They had just tried to submit an article for a publication to a major journal, which had been rejected. As a result, morale was low, and the team were largely giving up on the idea, thinking it too difficult. Now for me, I had just come from another assignment which also had 'publications of scientific articles' as one of its key objectives. As this was a very well-funded enterprise, we had the support of a highly skilled communications company doing this for our business. The leader of this company, Magda, was highly experienced and, frankly, an expert at managing the publication process. Over the time that I'd had the pleasure to work with them, a large number of publications were churned out for that business rather matter-of-factly. My unexpected knowledge of the area humbly reminds me of the great words of Sir Isaac Newton in his letter to Robert Hooke in 1675: 'If I have seen further, it is by standing on the shoulders of Giants'.

As I had worked hand in hand with and was guided by the giants of Magda and her team, in my mind, this was a very possible thing to do. We agreed amongst ourselves to give this one more shot and selected, in this case, an easier journal to gain access to, following the guidelines and Magda's process very carefully. To the team's surprise, their publication was accepted, and our first publication became a reality. Apart from illustrating what a low-difficulty, high-impact project looks like, there were also some other lessons from this case. 'Nothing feeds success like success.' It's amazing how a breakthrough can stimulate a team to new heights. Fresh off the heels of this success, that same team would go on to publish over ten publications over the coming eighteen months. They would even win an industry award for one of them. In fact, one of the later publication ideas which were presented to me was targeted for a highly ranked scientific journal. To be frank, when this idea was first pitched, I myself had my doubts and wondered if the team had gone too far. However, so as not to demoralise them, I gave it full support, and lo and behold – it was accepted on its first pass!

The next lesson from this case, I want to be careful in stating to avoid being perceived as arrogant. Arthur, one of my greatest managers of all time, once said to me, 'Great leadership is relatively simple. Just show the team the way and then get out of the way.' Getting out of the way is the most difficult and rarest quality to find because it is so counterintuitive. Before you think that is a subtle way of saying I am a great leader, honestly, it was only possible because I stood on the shoulders of many giants over the years, and the credit wholeheartedly goes to the them.

Another example which illustrates these principles and then some comes from Hollywood. I once watched a YouTube interview of Jason Walsh from Rise Nation, who is a trainer of Hollywood stars, especially when they are coming to play roles where they need to be superheroes (https://youtu.be/y5-R-TICKSw). In this case, it was Brie Larson training for her role as Captain Marvel. Brie made a comment to Jason that she had never achieved a pull-up before, and he took that as one of the goals of the training. Jason made the point that if they could achieve a pull-up together, it would achieve two key goals. First, creating the strength required to perform such a complex compound movement would build the body up to that superhero physique. Second – and perhaps unexpected – because it was largely deemed to be impossible, it would also do a tremendous amount for the mental state as well, imbuing a sense of confidence that is also needed to be a superhero. The case is also a great example of how difficulty is in the eye of the beholder. While it was seen to be something impossible in Brie's mind, Jason knew he could easily help her achieve it as he had already done so for so many others.

Inspired, I took on Jason Walsh's philosophy in my own personal training and asked my coach to target doing a pull-up for me as part of my exercise routine. For me at that time – and for pretty much all of my life – I could not even hang with my body weight for more than a few seconds (I'm talking low single digits here), let alone do a pull-up. It was, in my mind, pretty much impossible. Just to illustrate how impossible it was in my mind, the first time I had successfully achieved a pull-up, I almost had an anxiety attack. It was the first time I had ever seen the view from the top of the bars – almost surreal. There are a few lessons from the pull-up analogy that are interesting to apply here in our special project.

'Break things down into the smallest steps and begin executing.' We will discuss this in further detail again in the 'How?' chapter, but a pull-up is pretty much like a project. It's made up of different body movements/steps that, added together, culminate into that phenomenal orchestrated movement of the pull-up. When you break it down, there are clearly muscles that must be strengthened – biceps, triceps, the trapezius, and so on – each having their own specific isolated strengthening exercises. Also, when you analyse it more deeply, there are things you don't consider important but are clearly so – the core muscles. Further, there is the sequence of movements. When you go about working on these one by one without thinking too much about the end state, it can feel like Daniel-san from *The Karate Kid* waxing cars – demoralising. Having said that, with discipline, one day, when you look up, it will suddenly, almost miraculously be done, and you can view things from a completely new and different perspective.

'A beautiful sweet spot is one that is possible for you but impossible for them.' Like the publication example, the pull-up, again, is a very interesting goal because for most coaches, they have seen it done many, many times and have helped many of their students go from not being able to do it to doing it. For both the manager and the employee, this is one of the best things to identify in selection and why the project graveyard is a good place to look. Is there something that is so valuable for the other side or the organisation that is deemed to be too difficult for them (even impossible) but, in your sphere, completely doable? This is often just one of the absolute best projects to choose, just like the publication example above.

'Look for bypass-enabling mechanisms.' In this book, I use another example of how we created mobile apps to simplify and automate processes in our day-to-day work at an organisation I worked in. In the early days of that initiative lies another useful example of 'easy to do for one but difficult for another'. One of our senior executives at that time was very passionate about improving the speed and intuitiveness of receiving feedback from one of our key stakeholders. We had been doing this in an automated way, but it was done by email in a long and cumbersome manner. Her hope at that time was to make it faster and more intuitive through the use of a mobile app, enabling the survey to be done quickly anywhere. Bear in mind that this was in the early days of mobile and apps in general. At that time, there were a few 'master' apps that had been released that essentially enabled such things to be built and sent out white labelled via their platform. In the mind of this executive at that time, such a methodology required something to be built from the ground up as well as droves of IT personnel to make it happen. Often it is not necessary to build something completely from scratch if you can partner with someone else, outsource, or use these types of enabling technologies/software. I like to think of these strategies as 'bypass-enabling mechanisms'. During the course of one management meeting where we were discussing creating something like this and many people were saying it was too difficult, a prototype was created and sent to the team at that meeting, all in half an hour. All achieved thanks to a master survey app platform. It was met with enormous enthusiasm and surprise. Using 'bypass-enabling mechanisms', you can find more 'possible for some, impossible for others' outcomes.

Here's a project of another 'bypass-enabling mechanism' going back nearly two decades. We once undertook a research project looking at the effect of certain drugs on colorectal cancer, an ambitious initiative at that time because of our lack of experience and very limited resources. Sitting here today, recalling this, I not only grin at how simple life once was but also marvel at how quickly things evolve and improve. We conducted the research in one of the major cancer centres in the city that I was working in. In cancer drug research, one key outcome of particular interest is how long a patient is able to live after taking the drug versus without it, a term broadly used by the industry as 'survival'. The challenge with survival as a measure is the time it takes to follow up all the patients. Hence, at a given point when you stop your follow-up, not all patients would have reached the survival endpoint. To accommodate for this, a statistical tool called the Kaplan–Meier is used to estimate survival at the time you do the analysis (Figure 2).

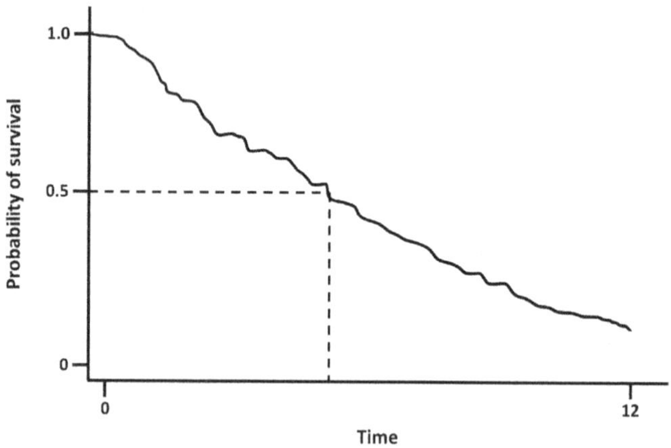

Figure 2: Example of Kaplan-Meier survival curve

As simple and funny as it sounds to the statisticians and researchers who may be reading, two decades ago in a small fledgling department, this was a big challenge. So we got to a point where we had gotten all the data and analysed what we could but were left with the final and potentially most interesting step of knowing the impact on survival. Going to established statisticians was going to take both time and resources we did not have. We found at that time a statistical software that was free to use. In those days, the word for it was 'freeware', and this software came with a manual and a function for Kaplan–Meier analysis amongst other things. From there, we had our survival curves, completed the project, and presented it at our scientific meeting as planned. This had a profound impact in the minds of the both the doctor and the department head at that time because it was largely seen as very difficult to do, requiring both high-end software and statisticians. It illustrates, in a different way, another useful tactic in finding and doing your project: see if a bypass-enabling mechanism like software can rescue a graveyard project. Thanks to advancement in technology, the software currently available to solve problems is simply mind-boggling in its breadth and depth.

I previously mentioned having cofounded two start-up companies, one of which was, in its early days, a sort of Uber or Grab for home healthcare. It has since morphed into other things which I will cover later. In the early days, we realised we needed an online mobile app booking system to manage the process end to end. We embarked on building one ourselves and, in short, failed big time despite having poured half of our initial seed funding into it. The idea was just too big and difficult to do. As a consequence, we went to a manual process, and over the years, the business morphed into something different – we began serving a more regular patient group in a narrow use case. Recently, with growth in the number of patients we were serving, we realised we needed to take another stab at automating the process. While we did not need a full end-to-end system as bookings were no longer on demand, there was still a need for scheduling and an app to shepherd the various stakeholders through the process. This time, rather than building the app, we went outside to look for ready-built software that met our needs and were amazed at the variety of options available and the expertise of those companies in adapting their solutions to our use case. As of the time of writing this passage, through a vetting process, we now have a top candidate and are planning implementation. I hope to be able to continue this story with good news in a future update.

Sometimes projects tend to be more people/stakeholder orientated. We have used a lot of software and technologically angled examples, so I don't want to neglect this important dimension. This example goes back even further in time to my days as a junior doctor working on the liver transplant unit, of all places. A particular patient still stands out in my mind very clearly because of the complexity of his case. He had both liver failure, necessitating a liver transplant, and severe coronary artery disease, requiring bypass surgery. Because of the criticality of both systems, it was deemed impossible to do those two surgeries in sequential fashion. If we did liver transplant surgery, he would probably have a heart attack and not survive the surgery. If we did the cardiac bypass first, his liver would tip into fulminant failure, also with a fatal outcome. As a consequence, we had to do a combined liver transplant and coronary artery bypass. I am cautious about using the word 'we' because as I was the most junior medical staff member of the team, my role was mainly administrative, a.k.a. filling in forms. To cut a long story short, the mammoth surgery was performed successfully, and our patient went home, life transformed. To this day, he still holds the record for the longest discharge summary I have ever written – and with a real pen, no less, not the fake electronic pencils you have these days! In those days, computers in hospitals were still very rare. This case illustrates the value of bringing groups of people together who may not be obvious choices of coming together – in this case, the liver transplant and cardiac surgery units.

As junior doctors of the liver transplant unit – and, in fact, for many units – one of our responsibilities was to take charge of our continuing medical education program for the department. I'm sure I speak for many junior doctors out there, but this is often one of the things we have to really crack our heads on. On this occasion, we chose probably one of the most common topics, which is to present an interesting case from recent months. So our combined-cardiac-bypass-and-liver-transplant patient was chosen. The unique thing about this case was that it required the two big units to come together to present it well. On that day, both heads of departments showed up, and we had one of the best sharing sessions ever, and I learnt several lessons. For starters, we don't take the time to reflect on things in many aspects of our lives, continually rushing from one thing to another, and there were indeed so many positive things to reflect on for this case. The second piece and the most impactful, something I did not realise until we got together, was having these two big units in the same room at the same time. My manager at that time was caught by surprise in a good way to have cardiac surgery with us that day. The cardiac surgeon was also surprised, and everyone enjoyed the discussion. Interestingly, both heads, who would normally leave early, stayed throughout, and we even enjoyed lunch over sandwiches together at the end. While it happened by accident, this is still, in my mind, the best of the sessions that I had organised in my hospital career. Herein, I believe, lies another interesting consideration: choose a project that's special because of the unique alignment of two or more not-natural partnering groups or groups at loggerheads with each other. Great things can happen, as it did in this case.

Despite my having said all this, you may indeed find nothing in your list that lands in that beautiful spot of 'low difficulty, high impact'. Then the next port of call is to go for 'low difficulty, low impact'. At the end of the day, success breeds success, and in many cases, small wins enable you to pivot to something bigger. The stakeholder survey tool is one such example. Its first version was created using a 'freemium' version of a software, but it served the purpose of proving that customer surveys could indeed be done via a mobile device and in a more intuitive way than the current method. Its purpose was inspiring the organisation to take things to the next level. So while the impact may be small for now, consider what it could be like if you were to roll it repeatedly. In a stepwise fashion, the impact would no longer be small after several iterations. We will cover more examples in the coming 'What?' chapter.

As you embark on your special project, be it something crafted by the organisation or something you came up with yourself, I want to give you some forewarning to prepare you mentally in the event that you may face some ridicule. It will be perfectly normal for people to laugh about your initiative, say how silly it is or that it will go nowhere. In fact, this is a good sign that you are on the right track! While this can be demoralising and make you think about quitting even without trying, please persevere. One has to be a bit focused here and utilise some selective hearing. To help embolden you, I want to share some of the ridicule that the greatest ideas of our time received at their first launch. At the risk of using too many iPhone examples – but it really is an incredible case study, and so many lessons can be learnt from it – here are some of the initial reactions to its first launch.

Bloomberg's Matthew Lynn had this to say about the launch of the first iPhone:

> The big competitors in the mobile-phone industry such as Nokia and Motorola Inc. won't be whispering nervously into their clamshells over a new threat to their business . . . The iPhone is nothing more than a luxury bauble that will appeal to a few gadget freaks. In terms of its impact on the industry, the iPhone is less relevant.

CoolTechZone.com had this to say:

> The iPhone is going to be . . . a temporary novelty that will eventually wear off.

Everyone's talking about electric vehicles today as well, so let's go back a bit further. Here's one on that other world-changing invention in 1904 from the *Carriage Monthly* magazine (https://www.businesstimes.com.sg/hub/bt-motoring/tesla-model-3-how-to-make-a-lambo-driver-cry):

> Humankind has travelled for centuries in conveyances pulled by beasts. Why would any reasonable person assume the future holds anything different?

There are many more where these come from. However, I do believe you get the gist. The things that we are discussing are simpler and easier to implement than either the first iPhone or the automobile, and looking at the authors who said these things, they are the ones looking somewhat foolish now. Thank your critics for the ridicule, see if there is any lesson to learn from their comments to adapt your approach, and then take heart that if it stands to be made fun of, the idea probably has some legs!

What Special Project?

This chapter is for the unfortunate scenario where there is no predefined or appropriate special project to take on. Well, actually, to be honest, I don't think it is all that unfortunate. In this case, you have to create one, and you have a whiteboard to do this. This can seem to be a daunting task, and having been in similar situations in the past, I want to recount a story from advice that Arthur, a previous boss, gave me and one which I have dished out for close to a decade on countless occasions.

Arthur had hired me for the second time in my career, but on the current occasion, it was at a new and different style of company while still in healthcare. It was quite a big culture change for me, and I must have looked bewildered for the first couple of months because during one of our scheduled catch-ups he said the following to me: You know, I hired you to do something different, something innovative and creative. I guess that was a bit of a vague and challenging request to understand. To frame it better, I want to make sure you understand what I'm asking to help you plan your next steps.

Innovation is frequently mistaken for two things – invention and discovery. Invention is like the light bulb being invented by Edison. Discovery is finding something that exists in the world but that no one has, as yet, found, such as Columbus or Zheng He discovering America. These two items tend to be very difficult unless you are in very specific departments or companies. So then what is innovation? It's actually tough to define, but perhaps it is best understood by looking at one of the most innovative products of our time: the iPhone. I don't think anyone would dispute how innovative and game-changing this product it. Having said that, to be brutally frank, when one actually looks at the iPhone, what is so innovative about it? It's a mobile phone, an MP3 player, a tablet, a touch screen, and a marketplace for software, amongst other things, but each of these components existed in its own form, in some cases for more than a decade, before the iPhone did. So what was so special and innovative about the iPhone? It was actually in the putting together of these different things and experience. For want of a better word, it is a rehash, a reshuffle of multiple existing ideas. I have used the words 'rehash' and 'reshuffle' to many of my team members as we have discussed the 'next big idea'. The iPhone never invented or discovered any of its components. It's special because of the way it put them together.

Based on this, let's move on to some more pragmatic examples of such 'rehashes' that have been successful. I once worked together with a team whose role was to be able to plan how to do research. It was considered such an important task because the 'how' determined the size, scope, speed, and importantly cost of doing such research, something that would make or break any innovative healthcare company. To do this, the team would review a large set of data in a manual and relatively ad hoc way that was actually quite individual dependent. Because of this, it was often difficult to convince key stakeholders about the outcomes of the forecasts and to make concrete plans. In a way, the team was performing a forecasting of how a project would unfold, much like a banker would predict the future of the financial markets to invest your savings.

After I discussed this with the team, we agreed that there would be value if we could standardise the process in a way. We did this by understanding past predictions, how they turned out, and what factors would favour a good or positive outcome. In so doing, the team identified patterns and created some common algorithms for the predictive process, something that was done in the heads of our teams but with great variation amongst the staff and projects. To make it more user-friendly for them to do the work, we built these algorithms into a working tool that was able to analyse all the data and present them in a structured way. This visualisation tool was also so 'cool', it was frequently used as a way to explain the outcome to stakeholders. We even gave the new system a name, which incidentally turned out to be my wife's name because the acronym of the process turned out to be such! The process which we used before our special project had existed for, again, decades and was functional. The data existed as well, although they would, of course, be continually updated as time progressed. All we did was utilise the data in a more structured way and put them together into a working and visualisation tool for users and stakeholders to consume the data. This may not be considered so fancy in today's world, but it was special at that time. It also made the process of planning faster and, by being consistent, enabled feedback loops that further improved the accuracy of our predictions. Incidentally, the tool we used was another 'bypass-enabling mechanism' example. It was software our company already subscribed to but utilised for other purposes. This made it that much easier to get the idea off the ground. It allowed the team to focus on the value-added activity of creating better forecasts rather than waste time on getting technology to work.

I want to highlight another project from further back in time for inspiration and consideration. This example is of an initiative we undertook around medical information. In the industry that I worked in at the time, there was a requirement for product manufacturer to be able to respond to questions from doctors, pharmacists, patients, and other stakeholders. This was a process broadly termed 'medical information'. This requirement still exists in the current day. At that time, we usually had a person or part of a person (i.e. this individual had other jobs as well) in every country responsible for this task who typically worked in isolation. As a consequence, the output was again highly individual dependent. Each person had their own way to answer their questions and their own pathway to getting help within the organisation. This led to not only inconsistency but also inefficiency of the process for the organisation. Their efforts were not typically tracked or measured, and as a consequence, no real transformational improvement was possible either.

Before we get into the project in greater detail, I want to highlight a few of the classic characteristics of this case that one should look out for in their special project: 'the power of small teams' and 'bringing groups of people together who may not be obvious choices of coming together'. At that time, medical information was not particularly sexy, and as a consequence, there was little interest in it, very little resources, very few people involved, and no big global initiative to latch on to. Because of this, the team members who worked in that department were also craving for support and help and were very willing to collaborate across different countries. This is the perfect storm!

'Break things down into the smallest steps and begin executing.' As I was discussing this with the team, it was clear that as the organisation grew and with advancement in technology, customers became more knowledgeable and had access to more information through the internet. As a result, queries were scaling in number, and it was becoming very difficult to respond rapidly, consistently, and in a high-quality manner. It was also becoming more difficult to resource the service adequately. In brainstorming this, we agreed that we should first target the simplest, easiest-to-achieve goal at making this process better. That idea, believe it or not, was merely creating a frequently asked questions (FAQ) document for each product and storing these items in a repository so that multiple countries could learn from one another, answer in a more standardised and faster way. We also stored everyone's responses in case the questions couldn't be answered by the FAQ so that others could benefit from them. This eventually served as material for FAQ updates as well.

Another wonderful outcome is that on a people front, it created a community for the medical information team to be a part of, driving collaboration further. Creating a FAQ and repository seems ridiculously simple, but this was unique at that time and delivered a meaningful improvement. It was another good example of rejigging, and just when you think that this is all it ended up being, remember the butterfly effect. The little flap of the wings of a simple FAQ would push Janice, the leader of this initiative, to further develop the idea, which resulted in, at the end, some years later, a full-fledged medical information processing system – a coordinated, high-quality way to respond, track, measure, and self-improve on such a critical process. For Janice, it would also mean an accelerated career that would put her in charge of a global organisation.

Another worthy strategy is to take a best practice from another geography and apply it in yours. I once had the privilege of working with a Hoake's disease (true disease blinded for privacy) patient society, who were working tirelessly to reduce the disease impact on the affected patients and their carers. Things that we take for granted such as driving, studying, and traveling were severely affected for patients afflicted with this condition. I had colleagues in another region at this time who had developed and run a program that essentially helped patients help one another – a 'train the trainer'–style ambassador program of sorts. With the help of a special communications agency, they helped patients craft and share their stories in a more compelling manner, stories that would help other patients in similar situations adapt and win over the challenges that their conditions placed on them. As coaching was not a natural skill for many, the program trained these patients to do better in this critical area of knowledge transfer. We helped them to be better coaches to other patients. Overall, this ambassador program illustrates a few good lessons in terms of what project to take on. Taking a project that is already well thought through, well received, and having an impact in another geography is often quite a safe approach to take. While one could argue that it might lack creativity, it makes up for it in providing a ready pool of supportive stakeholders and a reducing difficulty of execution.

Creating a program from scratch can be a difficult thing to do from the perspective of the need of time and resources. By lifting and shifting one, you only need to contend with language translations and cultural nuances, which can be challenge enough! The other great thing with 'lift and shift' is that if you can convince the program owner to expand to a new geography, you win over a group of stakeholders who can be very passionate as well as highly skilled in helping you succeed. This is their program, after all, and there will be a lot of skin in the game to want it to succeed. Another great lesson in this effort also came from my manager's manager, Hoch, in this initiative. In his efforts to cultivate 'creativity', a variety of ideas, including this particular program, was offered to me as out-of-the-box ideas to do something. This particular one resonated because of the positive impact we could make on patients. When we finalised the project choice, Hoch made a few calls to put the ball into play and got out of the way. We took it from there. If there is one thing I have learnt from great managers and giants, a key skill in great management is to ignite that fire of creativity, just nudge it in the right direction, and get out of the way.

We also cannot underestimate the impact of the initiatives that we take on. For this program, from very early on, we could see the transformation this training and coaching brought to the patients, imbuing them with newfound confidence and using that knowledge to help others. Over the years that it ran, it would have touched the lives of so many patients and the lives of their families. Honestly, it was beyond my expectation. In a tear-jerking moment, many years later, because of funding and strategic changes, funding for this project had to be wrapped up. When that happened, Dr Lau, the leader of the Hoake's disease patient society in the country we ran it in, sent me a message stating that it would now be taken over by them. Knowing how much it meant to me, he provided reassurance that it was going to live on. I saw in this incredible validation of the good that we were doing and how things could continue to take on lives of their own after we were gone. It's also an inspiration for the managers amongst you about the impact that you can have and the sustainability of things – something almost like a 'butterfly effect', where a mere flap of the wings through seeding an idea and clearing a bit of the way through a couple of phone calls can result in a life-changing, sustainable idea that will last long after you are gone. I'm sure Hoch had never imagined, as I had, that it would go on to a sustainable, nationally run not-for-profit program.

I also want to share two amazing things that happened on that project which may be more of a 'How?' chapter thing. We ran into many challenges along the way, of course, and this leads me to discuss some potentially touchy-feely matters that are just seen repeatedly when striving for good. If we are pursuing a worthy initiative earnestly, it is amazing how (and each of you may call it different things) the karma of the universe, religion, luck, fate, or destiny will help you along the way. First, we struggled to get an interpreter to be able to help us due to a host of factors: the scientific nature of the material, the time limitation, and conflicting projects. In that moment, I ran into (by the touchy-feely reasons mentioned above) a high school friend of mine who was in the country on a short-term visit to care for her father, a person whom I had not seen for a decade. This particular individual, Darleena, was perfectly bilingual in Chinese and English and had a master of science background to boot. Such a shocking meeting makes one a believer of otherworldly forces in play. We got to talking about the program and its challenges, and the rest is history. She took on the lead of the localisation and translation of the program.

During the course of the project, our lead project manager had to leave at a critical moment. At this time, we had just taken on Hannah, an intern, through the network of our country general manager. With very little choice because of the short time to launch, we passed on the work of the project manager to her. This is a classic 'a person fits the shoe that they are given' story. From her experience, the program would have been deemed to be well in excess of her capability. Hannah rose to the challenge, and between her and Darleena, we launched on time, on budget, and to excellence.

In these stories lies the inspiration for many a project. Nearly everything you do in the day-to-day or your team is a special project. If the process is big and common enough, just think about rejigging components to do the usual – faster, more accurate, with higher quality, and cheaper. Consider importing an initiative from another geography. Consider taking technology and AI to replace manual processes and systems, and starting with something simple is not a bad way. It is often these first small victories that spur further development and the beloved butterfly effect. And over a short space of time, the initiative is totally unrecognisable in its size and magnitude. Take that medical information project which started as a FAQ and repository. This led to the quality control of responses to measuring the time to respond to building a rudimentary system to manage the workflow to eventually a highly advanced IT tool to manage the entire process. One can also look towards common objections I've received in searching for inspiration.

'This is a global process/system, and we can't change it.' This is another excellent point, but rather than this being the reason why we never drive out of the garage at all, consider it as guidance on where to drive. To illustrate this point further, here are a few examples of things to avoid and things to consider as inspiration. In my line of work, there are many global rules or processes that govern the way we operate – and for good reason. For example, there are global rules for medical research that regulate things we can or cannot do to protect research subjects – definitely a good cause. Like many such global rules, they do have the danger of falling a little on the dreaded path to hell, leading to inefficiencies that do sprout up that could be targeted. However, as they would challenge a critical industry-wide rule, such projects should probably be avoided at least until we become a bit more senior. :-)

We also have regulations to guide the use of electronic tools to manage our processes as another example. This is an interesting example because depending on the size of the initiative, you may still want to consider this. If your idea is to create an electronic tool to replace an existing manual process that can garner support from the right teams, such as IT and quality, to navigate the regulations, it may be worth considering. If you can't mobilise this support, then this project is in the high-difficulty category of the prioritisation matrix, and one should look elsewhere.

Having said all this, in every system, no matter how regulated, I have seen opportunities exist to make improvements that won't be controversial. One merely has to look. Here's another example which, while perhaps outdated in terms of technology, can serve as good inspiration. I once had the privilege of working for an MNC at their regional platform, and the team working here covered a very large geographical area. As a consequence, we were often traveling to meet stakeholders and customers. Liv, our operational excellence leader within the department, wanted to tackle our bulging communications cost. Now there are many governing matters here – the telco, the mobile contracts, company policies and the software – which are naturally hard to change given that they involve a whole organisation. However, how we used these technologies and the mix was up to each department and individual. These independent decisions could still have a significant impact on cost.

In the pre-change state, we used to take calls on our cell/ mobile phones while traveling, incurring extremely high roaming charges at that time. During this period, the soft phone was launched – essentially a laptop version of our desk phones that could be used anywhere in the world as long as we had a laptop and an internet connection. Liv's directive to each of us was to use the soft phone whenever we could. For example, in our hotel rooms or foreign offices, where interestingly without much additional convenience because our laptops were often open, we still took calls on our mobile/cell phones. Naturally, calls that had to be made in airports and taxis would continue with the cell/mobile as access to a laptop and Wi-Fi was not straightforward in those situations. This fairly simple change in behaviour led to a six-figure reduction in the annual communications cost of our department with no reduction in the quality of our work. Imagine the impact of the entire organisation following this process and what good the funds saved could do for so many things we want to invest in but can't because of the lack of budget.

In our debriefing meeting on the initiative, we also discussed lessons learnt and potential pitfalls, and I want to recount one key one here. Any initiative should not be penny wise and pound foolish. We shouldn't aim to reduce cost or create some sort of efficiency if it impacts important parameters for organisational health such as project quality and customer interactions. It is often easy to chase a false economy thinking we did good, achieving a saving, but in fact hurt the organisation in a more severe way, such as through losing key customers because of poorer service levels. In so doing, we follow the 'path to hell is filled with good intentions' concept introduced in the 'Why?' chapter. When choosing initiatives and then metrics/goals for the initiative, ensure that it passes the 'path to hell' rule and that it delivers actual good as well. Hence, we did not stop mobile communications completely. If a call needed to be done while on the road, it should still continue. Only if it was convenient to open our laptops did we transition. So many times, we were just talking on our cells in the comfort of our hotel rooms or offices with our laptops in full operation.

In the process of coming up with what project to do, the manager and employee need to dance together. It is not realistically possible to go anywhere with just one person driving. They both need to dream up ideas, debate the merits of each idea, and more importantly, support the effort to do so. Finally, they need to agree on one and commit to the execution once the project has been chosen, hence why I feel this is one of the most powerful units within the MNC. If this is replicated in sufficient large quantities in a large MNC, I believe you have your coveted flywheel effect and high-performing organisation.

How to Do the Special Project

This next chapter will spend time discussing cold, hard day-to-day tactics as well as broad strategies to get the special project done. To be frank, these are also very useful tactics and strategies for the day-to-day business as usual and can be applied more broadly. As such, this chapter will be a useful one to look at both throughout your special project and as you go about your usual job.

Let's start at a broad, forty-thousand-foot, foundational level – our general ways of working. If there is one major criticism of an MNC, it is that they are big, bureaucratic engines and very slow to move. If there is one thing that threatens their survival in the future, for me, this is it. Having said that, an MNC is essentially a function of its people. If we, as managers and employees, can identify opportunities to drive the agenda in a more rapid way and do so, the whole organisation also shifts in the way in works. A lot of critics will say that big MNCs have too many processes in the way, as we have discussed in the 'What?' chapter. However, opportunities are always present, and even if we only act on the ones we could influence and enough of us do that, a meaningful difference would already be achieved. We should spend less time blaming the organisation and spend more time taking action ourselves.

One of the ways of working that I have seen in successful teams, even in MNCs, is simply the level of urgency that they take to matters. I was once a very small part of a global initiative led by Paul, our head of project management, who was essentially trying to do this very thing, increase the urgency and accountability for the day-to-day. He introduced us to a book, *If Not Now, When?* By Greg Searle. It tells the story of rower Greg Searle who won gold in the coxed pair event alongside his brother Jonny at the Barcelona Olympic Games. He achieved this at the ripe old age of twenty, and by his thirties, it seemed at that time that his career was over. In 2010, now significantly older than the rest of the British rowing squad, Greg made the decision to come out of retirement and go for gold again at the London 2012 Olympics. The book tells this incredible journey that eventually led to him winning bronze as part of the men's eight and cementing his place in history. There is a mantra in the book – 'If not now, when? If not you, who?' – which Paul introduced us to and kept talking about. I did a bit of further research on this, and the earliest version of this proverb can be attributed to Jewish scholar Rabbi Hillel nearly two thousand years ago, although it has since been quoted and inappropriately attributed to such esteemed names as Ronald Reagan and Emma Watson. Either way, something that has lasted for so long and been used so repeatedly usually has a point.

'If not now, when? If not you, who?' I find this to be one of the most apt, relevant, and useful things to ask of each of us for every significant task that we do in a big MNC. As organisations grow big, it's understandable that just who is accountable or who is doing a particular task becomes confusing. As a consequence, it ends up in the ether as no one's task and gets delayed repeatedly with no end in sight. To emphasise the point, I want to share this cute story (multiple sources, no clear origin):

Whose Job Is It, Anyway?

> This is a story about four people named Everybody, Somebody, Anybody, and Nobody. There was an important job to be done, and Everybody was sure that Somebody would do it. Anybody could have done it, but Nobody did it. Somebody got angry about that because it was Everybody's job. Everybody thought Anybody could do it, but Nobody realised that Everybody wouldn't do it. It ended up that Everybody blamed Somebody when Nobody did what Anybody could have.

While funny, the story is making a critical point. When it's everybody's job, it's actually nobody's, and things will not get done, hence why I like smaller teams as this reduces this risk. Nevertheless, regardless of size, as individuals and teams, we should always ask the question 'Whose task is it?' and assign a responsible party. A key lesson for me is also not to misunderstand it as an individual and that every task is yours. That would be counterproductive as well. The key is that it is someone's and that someone is known and crystal clear about it, which brings us to the second part of the statement: 'If not now, when?' Like the other half of the statement, it doesn't mean everything must be done now. That too may be counterproductive. We should see if we can indeed do the task now as there is no time but the present. However, if it doesn't make sense for it to be done now, then this essentially translates to having a target finish time for whatever task is in discussion. If we walk out of every project meeting knowing who is doing what by when, honestly, I feel we would already be well on our way.

'Cultivate creativity.' As managers, we often get into the rut of being transactional in working with our employees. Things become day-to-day, mundane about this or that project and how it is going. These are important, of course, and should remain. However, we can set aside some time to think about more aspirational matters, especially those that I see as more systemic – that is, processes that effectively govern or affect a majority of or all projects. Can we do something, tweak something, that could make things more accurate, faster, or more efficient? As employees, can we also do the same? Get through the business as usual and give some thought about what it is, and you can improve on systemic matters and make a suggestion. For both parties, when someone is suggesting something, listen. Just like Hoch's example of the patient ambassador program, systemic things are like the medical information processes which govern essentially every country all over the world, although of course, we can start small in just one country or group of countries.

'Be open-minded.' It's very easy to avoid discussions of out-of-the-box suggestions and focus on the day-to-day because it's so comfortable, but here lies the double-edged sword. Listen intently to what your manager or employee is saying and see if there is a point. When cultivating creativity, you will end up hearing things that you don't like or feel cannot be done. Before being too quick to shut it down, hear it out and perhaps even let them try. It's like the old parenting advice of letting children learn from their mistakes, and if we are completely honest with ourselves, I have found more often than not that these so-called ideas which I thought were silly actually worked. A prime example is that great publication from the forecast team that I didn't think would make the high science journal. Fortunately, I kept my mouth shut!

'Prototype and don't boil the ocean.' As you will be trying a lot of new things, I have found something that start-ups do very well and that is also useful at MNCs – start small. Build the smallest version of the idea to see if it works before scaling. I will use examples that I have either witnessed or been a part of to illustrate this point. I was once in a project where we were creating technology tools and apps to automate or simplify tasks that our teams were doing on a day-to-day basis. When this idea was first raised, it was largely laughed at and ridiculed for being too farfetched and difficult to achieve. So when we came to creating our first app, we asked the team to find the simplest process to work on. The task that we first took on was a mundane but highly repetitive and time-consuming one, calculating the use of drugs that we were researching. Part of the work the teams did at that time was to assess how much of the drug was used and to account for any unused portions. This is important in research because we need to know that a drug is used correctly, at the right dose and also not misappropriated for other purposes. In essence, this first tool was a glorified calculator which could have been done on an Excel sheet, but our aim was, at that time, just to prove that a mobile app could be made. It did not matter how simple or how limited it was, and so our first drug calculator was created. Despite being rudimentary, it inspired the imagination of the leadership at that time such that we gathered further resources to go to the next stage.

This concept of digitising manual processes using IT tools and apps is a great one for the modern times we are in because of leveraging technology. It is a familiar theme in many of our projects of taking an existing process that is highly manual, labour intensive, error prone, or a combination of these and using technology to do them better. Let's now move on to the next stage of this app story. As this was conceptualised to be a big complex project, we started with smaller examples such as what we had presented earlier about the survey form and drug calculator. We went on to create and launch other apps that would assess drug use, scan medications, and collect documents. Once proof of concept was achieved, this project would reach critical mass and was taken control of by our global IT teams. With their leadership and resources, such tools are now commonplace amongst the teams today.

Many of the original app ideas, while now much more sophisticated and high-quality, started from this original small crack team. The technology initiative also illustrates the amazing journey of a few individuals and the impact special projects can have on careers. Wanda held essentially the same position as Thena from the 'Why?' chapter, although in a different organisation and country. As we went into the second phase of the project with increased resources, it was clear that a dedicated project leader was needed. Wanda was identified as a key talent and needing a stretch assignment. Like Thena before her, she seized a role with great uncertainty and moved countries. Grabbing the bull by the horns, Wanda went on to lead the project to new heights, launching the new tools described above. In the year after coming to Singapore, she even performed a one-on-one demonstration in the global CEO's office. This was an organisation with a size of over thirty thousand in terms of headcount, mind you, with around 10 grade levels separating the 2 of them, so no small feat. Now that's visibility. She also went on to present as the only foreigner at the annual meeting of the largest country in our region in front of some 1,500 personnel live – this was before the pandemic, of course. Today Wanda is a director leading a team as an expatriate for a big MNC in Shanghai. With this type of approach, I'm sure Wanda's journey is not over. Wanda's story is also an illustration of the solution orientation raised in the 'Why?' chapter. When she had been asked to take on the role, the initial proposal was that she do the project as well as reduced duties on her day job. Wanda counter-proposed, saying that it had to be full-time given the project complexity and if we were serious about achieving success. When I look back on our efforts, I realise that this was probably one of the best decisions that we made thanks to Wanda. Don't just say no, find out what you need to enable it to happen and ask for it.

As the project grew, Wanda also brought in a second-in-command to help her, Doug. Just as Wanda went on an accelerated path in her career, Doug would also go on today to lead digital at a large pharmaceutical MNC. You will see many similarities in the cases of Thena, Wanda, and Doug, and to me, it's not really a surprise. I do believe it is a validation of the value of special projects to accelerate development and careers.

'Reward [the] effort rather than the result.' My sister who is an expert on child development often touts this as a key factor to developing a high-performing child, and I do feel it is very applicable to our situation, especially on the manager's side of the ledger. In big MNCs, just like in many things of a child's life, the reward (and worse, the punishment) is based on the achievement of a clear result – a score, pass/fail – and herein lies the danger because it promotes highly risk-averse behaviour in organisations. As an example, a part of my team's work is to ensure that we follow the globally established rules and guidance for running medical research. When deviations occur, this is usually frowned upon and, in many cases, punished, although not deliberately. As a consequence, we end up breeding teams who must follow things to the letter even when they do not make sense and who dare not propose anything for fear of breaking the rules. As a manager, while it is not intuitive, recognise, acknowledge, and, where possible, reward well-thought-through ideas even if they do not result in successes at first. This was the case with our drug calculator app. To be honest, even for something so simple, it didn't work many times before we got a prototype to work. The prototype was also highly limited in the types of scenarios it could be applied to, but it did what it was supposed to – inspire management to invest in the idea – and from there, the initiative went on to achieve wonders.

'Kill failures quickly and move on.' This is another very critical part of the creative and entrepreneurial process that I have observed in successful businesses and especially start-ups. If one tries many things, it is expected that a number, if not the majority, will fail, but to be able to find that right one, we have to preserve resources to cycle to the next idea and then the next and not waste a moment of time once we realise something is not going to work. The lesson from those ex-Apple employees about 'taking as much time discussing the things we don't do as the things that we do' really resonates here. While it may feel counterintuitive to do, I have found it critical to be continually assessing the things we choose to do. Take time to review how an initiative is going, evaluate it critically, and close it down quickly if it is not really happening.

Let's take a look at another example. In this case, the team had created a new product for a rare type of cancer which had been bought by a lead customer. It had a lot of redeeming features: it was the first of its kind, it had a whole host of features, and it helped the lead customer in conquering the market they were entering. However, as the project evolved, multiple changes took place in the marketplace. First, technology evolved such that the original design of the product could now be made with lower costs. The customers in this space were also under tighter and tighter budget constraints, making them push for new methodologies. Lastly, the market for the product evolved into a new area. To draw a parallel, in a way, we were like Kodak film, although our case played out much more quickly. Film was a great product and did amazing at the start (well, their start was for many years). With the advent of digital, this changed, but Kodak management just found it so difficult to face the facts.

Our oncology product example (and Kodak film) illustrates a few learnings. First, a good idea initially may evolve, because of the change in market dynamics, into a bad one, hence the need for continual review. In addition, if you push on anyway, the longer you pursue a bad path, the harder it is to actually switch it off. Part of this is the development of an emotional attachment to the concept because it is your idea or the team's idea. Lastly, you fear the response of management to learn that it doesn't work out, hence the need to reward effort rather than failure. We had multiple opportunities to shut down the project and pivot resources and efforts to something new, but on each occasion, we decided to pour good money after bad, ignoring the signs, falsely thinking that things would get better and not wanting to admit the writing on the wall. Eventually, it got to a point where the product started losing money, and that ultimately became the catalyst to shut matters down. In hindsight, it could have been done earlier, and we could have pivoted our resources into something new. We then proceeded to pivot to a product utilising new methodologies for its manufacture. The irony is that this product also rapidly became obsolete with changes in the marketplace, and to our credit, it was promptly shut down when we realised this. This leads me to my last thoughts on killing failures – have the courage to do so, and for those of us in management, reward effort and please do not punish but rather learn from failures. As counterintuitive as that may seem, punishment may actually cause poorer performance with your teams, hiding or holding on to things that belong in the graveyard.

This leads me now to a nuance of leadership. Although I do hope this is a project with a small team, you will inevitably have to lead some people, whether directly or indirectly, to get your project done. Throughout this book, I have spoken about a large part of good leadership as finding good people, providing space, not micromanaging (for want of a better word), and not doing the work directly. However, this is one exception to this rule, and that is the situation that your team member or direct report is in. In some rare cases, a more directive micromanaged approach is actually appreciated. I had the good fortune of being in training for and subsequently became a huge fan of a framework called situational leadership (https://situational.com/situational-leadership/). I do strongly encourage you to take a look at the link here and also at other resources available on their site. The concept essentially states that the style of leadership ranges from a strongly directional, almost micromanaging approach (*telling* people what to do) to the far end of a pure *delegation* (hands-off). Rather than having a fixed style of leadership, a good leader should actually modulate. That modulation depends on the 'development level' or 'performance readiness' of that team member for the task you are asking them to do (Figure 3).

Influence Behaviours	Delegating	Participating	Selling	Telling
Performance Readiness	High	Moderate	Low Moderate	Low

Figure 3: Simplified Situational Leadership framework (adapted from The Situational Leadership® Model | Center for Leadership Studies / https://situational.com/situational-leadership/)

The right pairing of 'leadership style' or 'influence behaviours' and 'development level' or 'performance readiness' will result in phenomenal performance, while the wrong one will increase the probability of failure. Let's use a few examples to illustrate this. In the first scenario, imagine that you are asking the team member to do a task they have done before many times. If, as a leader, you take a directional micromanaging approach, telling them what to do, this will antagonise them tremendously. The right approach would be to delegate completely and be hands-off. As they know the task very well, the risk of failure is very low. That individual would also feel a great level of trust, ownership, and achievement, encouraging them to great heights. In the second scenario, imagine that you are asking an individual to do something they have never done before. In such a situation, completely delegating and being hands-off would actually be a dangerous approach to take. It would create anxiety given that this is their first attempt at such a task, increase the risk of failure (which would further demoralise the team member), and disengage them from the project. A directional micromanaging approach, telling them what to do and how to do the task, would actually be welcome by the team member in such a situation. It would lead them to success in the task, raise confidence, and ultimately increase engagement in the project. And of course, there are all the in-between situations for experience where the leadership style would need to be modulated accordingly.

A great lesson for situational leadership comes from a rather spectacular project failure. It interestingly took place only a short time before my formal situational leadership training, which is one of the reasons why I do feel otherworldly forces are often at play in life. Because of the freshness of this project failure, I had a profound 'aha!' moment at the training, leading to deeper internalisation of the lesson. Without it, the training may well have gone in the proverbial 'in one ear and out the other' direction. The project in question was very similar to the Kaplan–Meier curve one described in the 'Which?' chapter. It was a type of project which I had done many times over the years. In this case, we developed a research project to understand the use of our product in the face of new competition entering the market. I asked a team member, Dieter, to take this on. Dieter was a highly accomplished gentleman with a string of degrees and long research experience. However, he had not done one with the precise methodology this one needed. I had mistakenly assumed he knew how it was to be done, delegated it completely, and missed all the signs of bewilderment and frustration on his part because he didn't know how to do it. Several months into the project, with a fair sum of cash invested, we had to pull the plug and cancel. It created a fair amount of professional embarrassment and spoilt my relationship with Dieter, which took quite some time to recover.

Apart from the general lesson about applying the right influence behaviour/leadership style, I also learnt that the diagnosis of performance readiness often takes deliberate steps rather than making assumptions off a gut feeling. A lot of junior doctors reading this will be familiar with this old training drilled down by our professors and seniors – don't *assume* anything or you will make an 'ass' of 'u' and 'me'. In medicine, with a lot of decisions having an impact on life and death, the profession takes assessing data in great depth rather seriously, and if one doesn't know the answer, they should seek it out rather than assume. My learning on assumptions was further enhanced by strategy teams in the companies I worked for. In any form of long-term planning, you just cannot know everything, so a key part of any strategy is a list of assumptions that have been taken into consideration in building the plan. This served as a potent reminder that forecasts were not fact and allowed debate about the fundamentals of the plan. It also made us acutely aware of what the assumptions were and to be vigilant of changes to them.

The other big lesson from situational leadership is that each manager usually has a preferred management style or influence behaviour. Mine, for example, is more delegating and participating, hence why I ended up in hot soup with Dieter's project. Through luck, a manager may actually manage projects very well if they have the right team pairing to their influence behaviour. However, some humility is needed over our abilities; over the long term, an incorrect pairing will inevitably take place, hence the need to respect situational leadership – diagnosing the performance readiness of your team member and applying the right influence behaviour for it. Getting the manager and the employee together as well as establishing some foundational ways of working is a great start. We are now on the way. However, this is often not enough to make a project of significance happen. You need resources, and I cannot emphasise more firmly how important this is to maximise the probability of success of your endeavour. Today's world in an MNC is at the highest peak of resource scarcity that I have ever encountered in my whole career. Nevertheless, if you look closely, you will always find someone to join the motley crew.

One of my favourite places to find talent is interns from university – probably no surprise to all of you after reading Hannah's story in the 'What?' chapter. More and more these days, higher education courses have some sort of practical component requiring their students to spend time working in a real-world corporate environment. In many MNCs, there are already regular intakes for these students, and getting access is just a mere call/email to HR away. If none exist, for the new manager, this is a perfect time to get it going. One challenge with intern programs is they typically fall into regular cycles. This leads me to one of the lies I would like to dispel: the word 'impossible'. Most projects do not have the luxury of timing a nice intern cycle. If you need talent, invariably with effort, something is still possible. In one of my projects, I met with a similar problem and was told by HR that we were out of cycle and that it was impossible to get interns. One of the other on-cycle interns at that time overhead my frustration and asked if he could help. The next day, he brought me to meet the dean of his faculty. I talked about the company and what we were doing and received the 'I will look into it' look. This is often code for 'thanks but no thanks', and I left thinking that perhaps it was impossible after all. This dean emailed me two days later with several interesting candidates who did not apply in the normal cycle for various reasons and were now looking for something. Two weeks later, an intern was sitting working on our project when it was supposed to have been 'impossible'. This batch yielded three interns and started a culture of bringing interns in that department that now exists eight years later. Of the early interns who came into the team, three have ascended to the rank of associate director in the company, and another is about to graduate as a medical doctor – the amazing butterfly effect of finding a few diamonds in the rough, chipping away a bit of rock, and allowing them to flourish.

For us managers, one of our key roles is to find and cultivate talent. You can see why I have been so inspired by finding interns with my first salvaging the patient ambassador program in the 'What?' chapter. Besides interns, MNCs have talents looking for something different to do and have free capacity because a big project is cancelled or is potentially about to be retrenched unless something is found. Speak with department leaders and HR. You will be surprised by what you find. In my career, I have seen great talent come from all of the above categories. Thena and Wanda, whose stories you heard about earlier, were talents flagged as looking for something different to do.

While on the subject of building teams, I want to go back to that interesting article interviewing ex-Apple employees and what they learnt from their time there. Please remember the lesson about the effectiveness of small teams. When you go about building a team, remember that it's not an exercise in building an army. For special projects, it is more of a crack team of commandos. In most of the initiatives I have worked on, the core team size has rarely been more than a handful of people (read: single digits). This makes accountability crystal clear and limits the risk of people thinking someone else is supposed to be doing something. It also makes it easier to be recognised for your efforts – a key step which is the subject of the next chapter.

This leads to another 'how'. Talk about the project *all the time*. Create slide decks and other materials like newsletters to aid this communication. Create an elevator pitch about the project. So if someone boards the elevator with you on the twentieth, on the ride to the ground floor, you should be able to impart the crux of the idea of your project. I know not everyone works in a skyscraper, but the elevator pitch analogy is merely to guide us to have a simple, easy-to-deliver description, and as it progresses, update them on what your project is about. While this may seem simple, do not underestimate the amount of effort required to conjure up, write down, and commit to memory this whole pitch. You will be surprised by how effective this is to gather the support and resources that you need. In the 'So Now What?' chapter, we discuss specific strategies to make your presentations more powerful and impactful. Consider each opportunity to speak about your project as a precious opportunity to build a coalition. As such, make every effort to prepare to deliver an amazing presentation, both formal and informal.

If you are lucky enough, the project may have the resources of a large external consulting firm supporting it, and if it does, embrace it and don't be intimidated by their presence. Learning and gaining visibility from the project is one thing. Learning the framework, process, and discipline of a consulting company approach to a project is another fabulous benefit. These are skills that will always be useful to you in your career. In one of my earliest transformation projects, I had the opportunity to work with McKinsey & Company, and the lessons I learnt – especially around structure, the organisation of large amounts of data, and presentation – have stayed with me throughout my career. Some of these lessons will come in the next chapter.

The other benefit for both the manager and the employee working on unusual projects, if communicated well, is that you become known in an MNC for being willing and able to work on strange, ambiguous projects. I was asked by the global head of my department to run a transformational initiative for our department globally some years ago simply because I had done a similar but, of course, much smaller initiative for Asia Pacific. Incidentally, this was the project supported by McKinsey.

Special projects, by their nature, are also complex and ambiguous, and it can seem daunting for both the employee and the manager to know where to start. To this effect, I have always found ideas and solace in an old piece of advice from an old boss, Ernst: 'In the face of insurmountable challenges and not knowing sometimes where . . . the destination [is], cut the activity into the smallest pieces possible and just execute [them] one by one'. Even if you are not quite sure where it is going, over time, like a jigsaw puzzle, the picture will become evident. In the setting of a special project within an MNC, one of the most important facets to consider is stakeholders. A very good way to chop things down is to simply list down all the stakeholders as well as categorise and speak to them one on one. You will be surprised by what you glean from it, but more importantly, these one-on-one discussions, which should be more than just once off, are also part of the change process of whatever initiative you are working on. Just like the pull-up story we discussed in the 'Which?' chapter, by breaking down the muscles and working on them diligently, one day you will look up and find yourself in a place you have never been in before.

Speaking of stakeholder management, I once attended a training and sat through a case study at IMD in Lausanne regarding Nestlé and their GLOBE program, the global rollout of SAP (SAP SE is a German multinational software corporation based in Walldorf, Baden-Württemberg, that develops enterprise software to manage business operations and customer relations) in their organisation. It was a case study of many lessons, especially given that many special projects are, by their very nature, change initiatives. However, one part of an interview with the global lead of that project, Chris Johnson, has stuck with me ever since and is a best practice, in my view. Chris was talking about the early days of GLOBE and how he had encountered challenges in its implementation in Japan. A cultural counsellor taught him the concept of *nemawashi* (https://japanintercultural.com/free-resources/articles/defining-nemawashi/, accessed on 13 June 2021). Its deeper cultural concept is beyond the scope of this piece of work, but in a general Japanese business sense, it means 'building a consensus using one-on-one discussion with each member of a decision-making group'. I remember a project we had to implement, also in Japan, looking at digitising some processes with mobile apps – yes, a part of Wanda's project. We undertook a very traditional Western approach, engaging with large groups of stakeholders at the same time, often in big meetings, often introducing new concepts at the same time. The words of one of their senior leaders at an early meeting still ring in my mind many years later – 'This is a ridiculous idea'. He did everything short of storming out of the room, but he may as well have.

At that time, I thought the project was dead . . . but as I reflected on this, the words of Chris Johnson came back to my mind, and I shared the concept with the team. Sadly, I had forgot about *nemawashi* in the first pass of our effort but fortunately had the presence of mind to remember it after landing in the ditch. We then tackled each stakeholder one by one, never introducing strange new concepts at big meetings. Instead, those big meetings became nothing more than rubber-stamping, celebratory meetings. Everything had already been agreed on upfront. The project in question turned around 180 degrees. From being ridiculous, we were praised by this senior executive at a leadership meeting one year later, and Wanda got her presentation in front of 1,500 of his staff members. Importantly, what I found with *nemawashi* was that it is not only useful as a Japanese concept; it is useful in any big change initiatives in whatever culture. The team's initial reaction to *nemawashi* was not a positive one, however. They felt this would take so much time and was so inefficient. In a way, it was true, but after a tremendous amount of pleading, we agreed to give it a try. We discovered actually that what time is lost in the process is made up for in the acceptance and sustainability of the project later on, and proceeding stakeholder by stakeholder, one by one, is a nice way of cutting things into the smallest possible pieces. This is table stakes at an MNC.

This Japanese initiative met with an early failure – and a rather spectacular one at that, which again makes me recall another very useful piece of advice from my old manager Ernst. In many important initiatives, we are often asked to push boundaries and challenge the status quo, but often it's difficult to truly know where that boundary lies. His advice at that time is that a good way to tell is if you cross that line and bungle something, then for sure, you are pushing the limit. Now if you are continuously over the line, then you are simply too far, but the occasional mistake is a reminder that you are near the limit, and it's a good thing in general. Learn from it and press on rather than be discouraged.

Failures and disappointments will come often during the course of a special project. There is very little question about this. Expect it, anticipate it, and be prepared for it. It is critically important not to take things personally and beat oneself up over things that go wrong. In a moment of sheer frustration recently, Arthur, a very old manager and now mentor, sent me this quote from the amazing writer and poet Khalil Gibran: 'And God said, "Love your enemy," [and] I obeyed Him [and] loved myself'. I found great solace in these wise words, so few in number yet so much in meaning. We are often our greatest enemies. Learn from your mistakes and move on. I hope also with all the sharing in this book that you will be able to learn from my own mistakes and those I have observed in my experience, accelerating your path to success.

As this is one of the most difficult things to conquer in pushing a project through, I want to cite one more source of encouragement or way of thinking. A lot of disappointment, regret, and self-hating will come from decisions that do not turn out well or circumstances that evolve out of our control. Throughout this book, I have used some examples from

Apple and the iPhone as points of learning. For this last story from them, I want to look at their founder, Steve Jobs, who has always been quite a polarising character to me. Clearly, he was a challenging individual to work with, but there was no doubt of the value he created and certainly there are lessons to learn from his career regardless of your position on his leadership. Over the years, I have watched the incredible Stanford commencement speech he delivered in 2005 (https://youtu.be/UF8uR6Z6KLc). He tells of three stories, and frankly, all of them have great insights, so do watch the video in the link here. However, for this particular point, it's the first story and message: 'The dots only connect going backwards'.

As you go along this journey of the project, decisions will be made, and some may turn out, at least in the short term, to be mistakes, but you just have to trust karma, destiny, life, or whatever else that you believe in that things will eventually work out for the best, that the dots will only connect looking backward and not connect moving forward. It's only then that we will have the courage to make challenging decisions and navigate the uncertainty of pushing the envelope. Many of the stories here would say the same thing. Thena was within weeks of being sent back to her home country before she got her extension and promotion. In the months and weeks leading up to this, the dots were certainly not connecting for her. However, fast-forward five years, and she was leading a global functional division as an expatriate in North Asia; the dots connected very clearly. The same goes for Wanda. After completing her major technology project, there was an in-between assignment which had her career going sideways for her. In the year that she went through this wilderness, the dots certainly did not connect. However, today, as she is sitting in Shanghai, they are as clear as they were for Thena.

I want to circle back to the subject of stakeholders given its importance. Putting together the list other than taking the time and effort to think about it is actually not hard. Executing each discussion, again, is not all that hard. Having said that, in multiple projects, I have found one common issue with the list: there is always a group of people in the list whom we avoid – yes, the ones whom we dislike. Often the ones we dislike are actually the ones we have to spend the most time on and should be prioritised. Be mindful of this danger group and give them the attention that they need. This brings me to the tough question – just how do we deal with the stakeholders we don't like? This is a difficult area for me, but I have a few reflections. Understanding that they exist, knowing who they are, and acknowledging that you need to address them is a great start. Congratulate yourself, at least, for that. Now let's go on to more practical ideas on how to work with stakeholders whom you do not get along with and are trying to avoid.

'Listen. Really listen.' Stakeholders we don't like, more often than not, have something to say that's relevant and important. Because of our preconceived thoughts, we fail to recognise this and pay them only a lip service in listening. I am glad for the following lesson that I received early in life and which I continually have to relearn, a lesson on listening and how the thoughts of others are often far more useful to you than you would think. Many moons ago, when I was a junior doctor, our unit had a patient with terminal bile duct cancer, Jane. To make matters more interesting, Jane's daughter was a medical student at the hospital that I worked at, and I felt an obligation to do the best I could. I remember at that time, I had spent a good amount of time on cancer units and thought highly of my skill (albeit wrongly) in keeping terminal patients comfortable and retaining as much quality of life as possible. This particular patient was suffering from terrible pain, and in my wrongly perceived wisdom, I managed it with oral opiate drugs. In my defence, this is a very useful strategy and is highly effective in many patients. However, as in many things in life, there are always exceptions. In Jane's case, she suffered from terrible nausea and vomiting as a side effect of the opiate drugs. Most of us know what that is like from having a bout of food poisoning, and I can hands-down say it is a shocking thing to experience over a sustained period. To be fair, I was at my wit's end about how to handle this and certainly did not enjoy seeing my patient in such distress every day. One morning, as we made our rounds, we saw Jane, and my manager at that time asked me to get input from our palliative care team to see how they could help us. I remembered muttering under my breath at that time about how useless that would be and 'What does palliative care know?' He picked up on that because his words, I still remember many decades later – 'Ken, I am telling you to get palliative care. I'm not asking you. This is an order.'

I'm a good soldier, if nothing else. So I grudgingly called palliative care to come. That event, while over two decades ago, is as clear in my mind today as though it were just yesterday. Cathy, our palliative care doctor, came onto the ward. She had bright red hair and brought such an air of humble confidence to the ward that I could feel things were already different. She said hello to me, and we both went in to see Jane. I will be direct here – I had my ass handed to me that day. Nevertheless, I was grateful for it and learnt many great lessons, and Cathy, in her own butterfly effect, would have a positive effect on so many people because this story, I have told to teams and people I have mentored time and time again over the decades.

Cathy waltzed into the room just like she had done into the ward, like a bright ray of sunshine, went up to the bedside, sat down, and just held Jane's hand. She talked a bit but mostly just listened. The care in taking the time to listen, holding one's hand, and just showing care is more effective than many drugs. Honestly, anyone would have felt better just from that alone. It was incredible. Heck, even *I* felt better. I ended up holding a lot of patient's hands after that day. After Cathy took her time assessing Jane and understanding what was happening, we went back to the ward to look at her drug chart. At that time, I had been dosing Jane with generous amounts of oral morphine. While a fabulous drug for pain control, it can cause severe nausea and vomiting as a side effect, especially in its oral form, as each dose results in a peak of drug in the blood. Cathy advised me that the morphine was the likely cause of Jane's nausea and vomiting and suggested that we shift to a patch form of fentanyl, which is a drug that is in the same family as morphine, but because it is absorbed through a patch on the skin, it provides a more stable blood level of drug and can cut out the nausea and vomiting. It worked wonders because the very next day, Jane started to feel better. Her pain was under control, and yet she did not feel nausea and vomiting anymore.

It's hard to describe the impact this made to the patient, so I will tell it exactly as it happened. One day, during my usual day-to-day activities, I wandered into Jane's room. It was clear I had interrupted a moment. She was with her family, and there were smiles all around and even some laughter. I looked at them, and our eyes met. Despite there being no words exchanged, I had never communicated and received so much detailed emotion and messages in my life – thankfulness, gratitude, relief, happiness, kindness, sympathy. The gaze between me and the family was locked for a good moment; those messages were transferred between us, and I turned on my heel and left. Moments such as the one I had stumbled into are worth their weight in diamonds to a terminal cancer patient, and I felt an immense privilege to have been able to be a part of just one. That simple act of taking time, listening to the patient, and making a small change to their drug regime bought them more of these moments – a gift that is beyond value to measure.

Jane eventually succumbed to her cancer, but I still remember her case as one of my greatest achievements, albeit thanks entirely to Dr Cathy. While you may feel as a reader that death should not be something a doctor should feel happy about, in certain circumstances, such as for the terminally ill, the ability to be able to enable a few more of those moments is as precious a victory as curing someone. In moments when I think about what other paths my life could have taken, I do serious think a career in palliative care may well have been one for me. Here endeth the lesson. Thank you, Cathy.

Jane's case also teaches a few lessons relevant to the 'Which?' and 'What?' chapters, the most significant of which is that sometimes very small things are all that is necessary to achieve success. Just like the survey app and Kaplan–Meier freeware stats tool were so simple, in this case, a simple change of giving the same drug family from oral to a subcutaneous patch form was all that was needed to change Jane's life – a simple rehash or rejig of essentially the same thing. The other is to reach out to others for help, in this case a human being in the form of Cathy, our palliative care doctor.

'Tender loving care.' Another story from early in my career took place on a busy weekend afternoon in the emergency department. On this day, a patient by the name of Natalia came in. She had been suffering from chronic pain for most of her life, and in recognition of this, her file was as thick as an encyclopaedia. So on this fateful day, Natalia had come in complaining of her generalised body pain which had been going on for years and was no worse or better that busy afternoon. Now weekend afternoons in emergency are crazy places to be, and let's just say tensions can be on the high side. I was tremendously frustrated with Natalia because in my mind, she had come in at the worst possible time to the wrong place as it was emergency. As things had not changed, I just could not understand why of all times, she had to present now when we had car accidents and heart attacks to deal with. We naturally got into an argument, and Natalia was feeling very upset, not wanting to leave. Ahmad, one of my ex-bosses who was a surgeon, overheard our argument, peeked through the curtains, and said again something that haunts me to this day – 'Ken, TLC. Ken, TLC' – and he just left. Now surgeons are not exactly known in general terms for their bedside manner, preferring instead to make up for it in their hand skills. However, Ahmad had the extraordinary insight to know what to do and pass me the message – show your patient some tender loving care.

It clicked a switch in me because I became a lot more empathic with Natalia. I didn't hold her hand but certainly took time to listen to her, to sympathise with her, and essentially told her I understood her pain and concern. The conversation completely turned. Natalia became a lot more relaxed, stopped her complaining, and said she was feeling better. She left emergency that day feeling better and honestly, I believe, with less pain. For some of you reading this, you may feel I did not do anything. However, the act of listening and showing empathy can be more powerful than the strongest painkillers. Such was the case with Natalia. This is a little like the book *Men Are from Mars, Women Are from Venus*. One of the lessons here for improving relationships between men and women is the difference in our expectations. Men typically want to jump in to fix things in a very visible and physical way. For women, their expectations are different. Being heard, shown empathy – that is as meaningful as, if not more so than, bigger actions that fix the problem. In engaging your difficult stakeholders, take time to understand their concerns, listen to what they have to say, and above all else, try to relate to their issues. It is amazing what insights you can derive and how much trust and how many relationships you can build just by doing so.

'Go outside of the environment.' Another strategy that can be applied to challenging stakeholders is to take them outside of their natural environment where there is a normal instinctive reaction to battle you. A venue like a coffee shop or restaurant for casual lunch can really defuse a situation if you can find some common ground outside of the project that you are working on. In one of my previous roles, I was at loggerheads with our legal department head. This is a natural tension as crazy ideas tend to be associated with risk, and our lawyers are naturally trying to contain risks. The situation continued to deteriorate to the point where in one meeting, I un-customarily lost my cool and stood up and raised my voice. I was reflecting this to Wolf, my coach at that time, and his advice was precisely this – go outside of the environment. He felt that things had deteriorated to such a state that the only chance was to build things from the ground up. I found out from colleagues what cuisine she liked and asked for us to catch up over lunch. When you do something so unexpected, it already resets the matter. I remember that day, when I was coming over, her eyes nearly rolled over to see me at the door of her office. However, when I asked that we merely go for lunch, it was very hard to battle that. I can tell you that I dreaded having to do this for days. Prior to going to her office, I paced mine for a good number of minutes before I mustered the courage to do so. Surprisingly, we enjoyed our lunch together. We found common ground and, from there, had a very close, collaborative relationship that would last throughout the rest of her time at the company.

'Send A to see B.' At the risk of sounding too much like a fairy tale, a long time ago in a land far away, I attended a training on change management. As part of the course, we played a computer simulation on implementing a change initiative in a large MNC. The simulation had a variety of tactics that could be deployed to facilitate the change – town halls, meeting with the CEO, newsletters, meeting with department heads, gift packs, focus group meetings... you get the idea. One particular tactic has stayed with me over the years and is almost always something I consider in engaging a difficult stakeholder: 'send A to see B." The idea behind this is to give thought around who is the messenger you send to address this stakeholder and not just focus on the content of the message. While the message may still be the same, the level of acceptance or cooperation received can be heavily influenced by who we ask to deliver it. A stakeholder can be more willing to listen to someone of authority or position, who went to the same training or university, comes from a same background or geographical area or some other type of connecting force.

The following real life case is a great example of this type of strategy. As per my usual routine, I arrived for work at the hospital ward early one morning. This morning would be different however, as I was met with one of my patients going into an emergency situation. In such a scenario, we typically call a "code blue" in the hospital, summoning key emergency critical care doctors and staff. When the emergency team arrived at the scene, I was asked to give a brief about the patient. Despite giving what I thought was a succinct and precise summary, it was almost as if I was not present and had said nothing. My boss arrived moments later and when he was asked about the patient, said almost the same thing as I did! Despite being the same words, more or less, it was met with urgency, reverence and acknowledgment by the emergency team. Given his seniority, in this situation, he was the right A to see B. While I was offended by this incident, I later recognised that rather than lament about this law of the universe, the time would be better spent taking advantage of it by figuring who should be the A.

Another example of this strategy at work comes from popular culture in the Terminator series. This classical piece of science fiction tells the story of how artificial intelligence (AI) becomes self aware and proceeds to exterminate humans, believing them to be a threat. The humans would eventually fight back and win the war through the leadership of a messianic figure, John Connor. In an effort to change this outcome, the AI would send robots called Terminators back in time to kill John at various times – pre-conception by targeting his mother, as a child and as an adult. In one timeline, one of these Terminators, model number T-800, would be captured by John's future self, reprogrammed and sent back in time to protect himself as a boy. In so doing, John would develop a relationship with and soft spot for this T-800 machine. The AI would in one timeline succeed in assassinating John by taking advantage of this soft spot and sending a T-800 to do the job.

'Meet just for the sake of meeting.' Erica, one of my previous sales managers, was always meeting someone or the other for coffee and lunch. I asked her what was so important that she always had to be doing that. She passed on to me one of the most useful tips of my customer management career – in building your relationship with your customer, 'you should meet them most of the time for no reason other than to just meet them'. She felt that most of the time, like what I had done with the legal team, we only see them when we need something. How on earth, according to her, is that the basis and foundation of a good relationship? So Erica says that she is constantly meeting up with people for no reason because on the day when there is good reason, it becomes easier to ask for what you need. I think Erica was simply the best at this stakeholder management 101, and whenever we had an issue with a customer, she was the first person we called upon.

Once you have your stakeholders, start meeting with all of them, and if possible, meet when there isn't anything required as well. You will also be surprised by how disciplined execution works – one thing after another – how things eventually happen. You feel like you are going sideways until suddenly, the work takes flight. Some years ago, in launching a new product, we were attempting to get it reimbursed by the national insurance in the biggest hospital group of the country I working in. I remember at that time visiting Dr Ho, a key decision maker for this drug class many times, explaining the merits of such a product for their patients. Meeting after meeting ended cordially but without any action at all. We really felt like we were going sideways and not making any progress at all. At one point, we had given up, and we then progressed to meetings for no reason at all, speaking about everything from children's university education to craft beers in Tasmania. One fine day, out of the blue, he called the team to come to see him, and to our surprise, when we walked into his office, he had the application for reimbursement form on his table. I was expecting that he would need help justifying the reasons for reimbursement, but to my surprise, he filled in the form right in front of us. He coyly asked if these arguments were indeed correct. So he had been listening all this time! The submission was made, and reimbursement took place a few months later. This was a great example of the diligence of plan execution and patience as well as meeting for no reason at all.

'It's the beginning of a beautiful friendship.' Once in a while, you will find that meeting those you don't like can be the start of something most unusual. My best friend, when I first met him, I disliked tremendously. You could almost say I hated him. I felt he was obnoxious and irritating and arrogant. However, circumstances pushed us together, and in having to get to know him, I found redeeming qualities that make him an incredible best friend – kindness, insane loyalty, and unconditional support, just like the lawyer in our previous example, who could have ended up as an enemy, became a mutually respected colleague. Aside from moving the project forward, tackling our most dreaded stakeholders can yield tremendous rewards in unexpected ways.

'Feedback is a gift.' As you go along on your project, it is going to be essential to align regularly with the team and stakeholders. As both manager and employee, you are in a position to provide feedback to help one another improve. Otherwise, the base state is some comments but usually negative ones – or worse, no feedback at all – so everyone is flying blind. Arthur, whom I have quoted so often that many will remember him as one of my wisest managers, shared some more amazing words on the topic from the amazing writer and poet Khalil Gibran: 'Between what is said and not meant and what is meant and not said, most of love is lost'. Too often in meetings, it is indeed the things that we don't mean, uttered in the 'heat of the moment', that are remembered. When good things happen, we don't think to just say it.

I will tell you a personal story now, but it also illustrates many scenarios I have seen played out at a corporate level. During one of my coaching sessions with Wolf many years ago, he asked me about my grandfather because I often spoke about him and shared stories about how he helped me develop and become better. He asked if I ever told him how I felt or told him that I loved him. My instinctive response was 'Awww, Grandpa knows that', to which he replied, 'How will he know if you don't say it? Can he read your mind?'

This is actually the most common response when I quote Khalil Gibran in my mentoring and coaching of others. They should already know. I came up with all sorts of excuses not to do this with my coach, and finally, he twisted my arm with the following: 'If saying it is so difficult, then just write it down, Ken. Please do it. Time is limited'. So one day, after breakfast, I wrote my feelings down in a letter to my grandfather. I went over to his place and gave it to him. He was initially puzzled to receive a letter in this manner and, upon opening it, spent an extraordinary amount of time reading it. He looked at me with a few flecks of tears in his eyes – only the second time in my life for me to see that – and like the earlier moment in the story of Jane, we had a moment. We proceeded to have lunch together, and when he retired to his room, I remember him dashing out, asking his nurse where his letter was. It was brought to him, and he promptly placed it in his drawer of precious things. I told him in that letter that he had been the best grandfather and that I loved him and thanked him for everything he had done for me. It was clear, even at his old age, not only how meaningful it was for him to read the letter coming directly from me but also how therapeutic it was for me to be able to do this. He passed away at the ripe old age of one hundred some years later. Because he was so close to me, I always worried about how I would be able to let him go. Having done this enabled me to reach closure. This is a very deep and personal story, but I wanted to share it to be able to emphasise how powerful feedback can be and why it must be done.

So to the response that 'they already know', my point is how do they know if you don't tell them? Are they mind readers? Even if they do know, it can still be profound for them to hear it or read it coming directly from you. Just imagine the energy and encouragement this can provide to the recipient to soar to greater heights. There are many frameworks for providing feedback, and it is beyond the scope of this book to cover them. Frameworks such as 'Situation, Behaviour, Impact' (SBI) and 'Feed Forward' are ones that I like. I encourage you to seek them out.

Some of you who have worked with me and are reading through this book will find some of this surprising. Some of the advice will seem different to what you have heard or wasn't applied in similar situations that you were facing. One reason for this is that I may have not yet learnt that lesson by the time we encountered your challenge. For obvious reasons, I won't discuss this reason any further. The other is something that warrants some discussion and is the cycle of learning, forgetting, and relearning. What I have learnt over the years is that learning new things is essentially at par with relearning important but forgotten lessons. As time passes by, after learning an important lesson, it's natural that it is no longer at the forefront of your mind or, worse, forgotten altogether, so much so that when you encounter the same problem again, it's almost as though you are encountering it for the first time and making the same mistake all over again. The

GLOBE program and *nemawashi* is a wonderful example. My time at IMD preceded the Japan project by years! I have encountered that over the years, and this is one of the reasons for writing this book – to scribe all the lessons in the one place, to be able to look through them again, to remind us and to help us address new problems, a little like note taking in meetings. As you learn critical lessons, read useful literature that resonates with you - find a place to put all these so you can refer to them when the time comes. When the time comes, remember to at least take a quick look at your treasure trove for inspiration. As I prepare for my new role, in a way, this book serves as an aide-mémoire of pretty much every lesson and tactic I have learnt in my entire working career and life for ready application to the new organisation's challenges.

As we reach the tail end of this chapter, I want to wrap up with some more basic granular tactics that are equally effective at getting to your goal. As you progress through the project, you will encounter things that will drive you a bit mad – responses from individuals, unexpected roadblocks, illogical arguments. With the availability of rapid response tools, it is tempting to lash back immediately. This advice is simple: don't. Never respond in anger; you will regret it later, more often than not, and make the situation worse than it already is. Fairly early in my career, one of my senior eccentric mentors, Rob, whom I admired greatly, used to say to me, 'You youngsters just respond so quickly and so much, creating a horrible amount of unnecessary movement. In my day, correspondence was dictated, typed up, sent for review, edited, reviewed again before being sent. A process that took days.' Rob used to say that in many cases, he was shocked by what he had written when angry. Fortunately, the slowness of those ancient processes meant that these correspondences could be retracted before being sent out, quite unlike the email and instant messages of today. In many of these cases, Rob said, these angry responses were never sent, and further incident was avoided. He even went on to say that in fact, no response was actually necessary, and the effort to create a response was a complete waste of time that could be invested into more value, creating parts of the project. Rob's last point was that if indeed a response was needed, then there was actually no harm in waiting day or so to respond when we were more level-headed – wisdom.

To add to this wisdom on emails, an old manager, Ernst, made a major point to me early in my career. Emails are only for short instructions or the documentation of decisions. More complex explanations or instructions via email are fraught with the danger of misinterpretation because we now work for global organisations with cultural differences and, with that, the fact that not everyone reading your note would be native in that language. Anything that required more than three sentences to explain would require a phone call or verbal meeting so you could indeed verify understanding and read body language for agreement. Most of the team members who have received this advice from me cringe at the time required to do this, especially if it meant talking to a dreaded, disliked stakeholder. However, like the *nemawashi* advice earlier in this chapter, in my view, the investment of time pays dividends well in excess of the effort in the initial period. I have seen so many misunderstandings lead to much larger time wastage trying to 'fix' things later on, just like the example of our Japanese project. Just pick up the phone...

The other point for me to make which is somewhat related is not to respond or make decisions when tired. When working on special projects, you will likely be working very hard, and there will be times when fatigue sets in. Make sure you get as much rest as you can and avoid making decisions in a state of exhaustion. The best learning of this, again, goes back to my days in the hospital. In those days, it was quite common for doctors to have to do shifts of twenty-four hours straight and greater in many countries. There were plenty of moments wherein, when I reviewed a day after resting what I had ordered in the wee hours of the morning of a long shift, I was shocked at the quality of my decision making.

A great example of this is a very sad story, but I will tell it to emphasise my point. Junior doctors usually work in a major training hospital and are rotated to work short assignments over a few months in country hospitals to support the broader healthcare system. Usually, at the end of a shift, many of us are understandably keen to rush home to spend time with family and friends. On one fateful morning, one of our colleagues, who was also a family friend, made the decision to drive home after doing one of these infamous twenty-four-hour shifts, desperate to get home to be with family. He fell asleep at the wheel, drove off the road, and died crashing his car into a tree. Most of us would be stunned by what would possess him to embark on a two-hour drive home in such a state of sleep deprivation. However, that would be us in a normal, fully rested state of mind. Convert that to exhaustion after twenty-four hours of working and desperation to be home, in the comfort of our own beds and near family, and our decision making would probably not be as sound too. Fortunately, conditions have improved greatly for doctors in many of the countries I have worked in. While it was a terrible tragedy, some good came out of it as our professional association acted to reduce working hours as a response.

This friend of ours was not an isolated incident, but I will stop the dark stories here so as not to sour the flavour of this book. Interestingly, this is one of those lessons that I have had to relearn and relearn over the years. Fortunately, all it takes is for one of these dark stories to be brought up by a friend or relative to flick the switch on. 'Do not make decisions when tired.'

So Now What?

At this point, we have now covered most of the very important aspects of finding and running a special project well. Despite all this effort, the race is not yet finished. In this last chapter, I want to cover the topic of communication in much deeper detail. It is relevant throughout the project, and we discussed it briefly in previous chapters. However, it is especially important as you reach the end. In fact, *communication* is probably not quite accurate as a word. I am going to call it (a bit more provocatively here) 'advertising' and 'positioning' or 'showing off' just to emphasise the point. Showing off cannot be underestimated, and this is a critical step. Of course, the aim of this project is to improve performance for the company and, depending on the type of business, the customers and the world benefits too. However, it's reasonable for the individual and their manager to expect to benefit from it directly career wise so that they can move on to more significant positions and take on bigger, more impactful projects.

Here, I want to share an example of a real-life case. One of the companies I worked for in the past underwent a merger. Part of the reason for this merger was to be able to utilise the combined capabilities of both companies to produce better products with less errors. Shortly after the merger, a project was put into place to make this objective a reality. On all accounts, this was a perfect project to choose. My colleague, whom we will call John, took on this project, led it for Asia, and had clear ownership of the project despite it having many actors – a key feature which we discussed in previous chapters. It was also unusual to have this clarity for something so big. To lay further groundwork on this case study, let me describe the grading system of the company we worked at. For simplicity's sake, the highest grade in the company for the Asia region is Grade 10. John was at Grade 8 when he had taken on this special initiative. In my past experience, I have seen that for a project of this level of impact and visibility, this should have gotten John a promotion to Grade 9.

The project ran very well and did deliver on its objectives. However, while John's department and responsibility grew post project, he did not achieve the promotion that he desired so much. When I look back on the outcome, I feel that there are two key lessons to learn related to the key focus of this chapter. The first is adequate volume and breadth of communicating the project and, in essence, 'showing off'. John felt that all he needed to do was keep the global project owner happy and did not feel the need to do broader communication beyond the required standard business updates. The global project owner was certainly happy with John's work and very influential in the organisation. However, despite all this, she had less say in what happened for promotions in Asia where John was based. Many stakeholders were insufficiently communicated to or left untouched. In many cases, John felt that these stakeholders were not relevant to his project. While this is true in a purist way, many of these stakeholders were executives in Asia who did have influence over promotions. The theme of combined capabilities was also of great interest to other business lines, and there was interest to have John help out in these areas. While he was correct that this was deviating from the focus, towards the later end of his project, he could have been more open-minded and pivoted. Some of these business lines were headed by executives with a lot of Asia influence. It's a little like the medical information project we discussed. What started as a FAQ and repository pivoted all the way to a global technology system. The leader of that initiative could have stopped at a FAQ, but thankfully, she didn't. That continuation and pivoting to bigger and bigger things led, naturally, to her accelerated career.

This leads to another important point. In many cases, people say that it's unbecoming to be showing off and that the company should recognise their efforts by itself. This is a little like the example in an earlier chapter on how companies should plan careers out better. It's a great point, without question. However, rather than blame the organisation, one needs to take action. It's hard to change the company, but you can control your own individual actions, and making appointments to update stakeholders on the project is well within one's control. The great thing about a special project is that it gives you an excuse to engage a broad range of stakeholders and help build your network.

Another excuse often raised is that people are not interested – once again, a fair point – but it should not be a reason not to do anything at all. For starters, it's rare to have *no one* interested at all. In many cases, there is an interest from the stakeholders about what is going on for a project. For John's project, this was a key focus area, and there truly was intense interest from other business owners. Also, updates don't have to be done formally. They can be done casually over coffee or lunch or through simple emails or newsletters. In many big MNCs, multiple forums like town halls and management meetings exist where people can essentially just volunteer to present. These forums are often short on volunteers because too many people also feel that the organisation should do this for them, but an organisation is nothing if not the sum of its people. By taking action, we are acting and making the organisation more like what we want and expect. Communication is a lot like speaking slowly in your presentation. If you feel you are communicating too much, it is only then that it is probably at the right level.

'It takes too much time.' This is another objection I hear frequently and is like the one I hear for the *nemawashi* example. But if it's worth doing the special project, it's worth taking the time to do it right all the way to the end. I want to come back to discretionary effort but, in this case, to raise it for the individual. Usually, by this time, good amounts of your blood and sweat have been expended on the project. Having gone the extra mile and applying all that discretionary effort, don't you owe it to yourself to finish it right and claim the prize?

This also brings to mind teachings from an old athletics coach from my younger track and field days (note that I was hardly an athlete but was a fairly quick runner). I remember, on more than one occasion, finishing a race lower in position than expected because I had slowed down before the finish line. My coach at that time used to say that the real finish line is actually several meters past the visible finish line. It's a nice analogy to apply to the finish of a project. The true finish line in your mind should be several steps after the obviously visible finish line. A special project is not complete until you communicate it extensively and plan the next steps.

In addition, sometimes the prize needs to be claimed, but it may not be exactly in the format that you expect.

The outcome of this John's combined capabilities project necessitated many global positions to be put into place. However, John did not compete for them as they would have required relocation to other countries. These would have been positions of significant influence that would have gotten him his promotion. It's difficult for me to comment on John's personal circumstances, and these may, of course, well outweigh a promotion. Nonetheless, this would have clearly been an opportunity to advance. In the cases of Thena and Wanda, moving countries to areas of need were clearly key success factors in their accelerated careers.

While we are on the subject of impact, I also want to highlight the flexibility required in assessing this key component. Working on special projects is like working in a start-up; you have to be flexible along the way, adapt your approach, and modulate the project based on data you gather or changes in the environment. Very often, the end may not be as expected, but you must not jump too quickly to the conclusion that it is a failure. If we look at any project in the right way, some impact has been made, and it is essential to understand this and communicate it. An example of this is a start-up that I co-founded with some friends and mentioned earlier in this book; where we essentially wanted to create an Uber for home care. When we first started, the aim was to create a moneymaking unicorn startup company while adding value to the whole transition of healthcare from big institutions to the home. Bear in mind this was quite some years before the COVID-19 pandemic. Over time, this initiative morphed into a social enterprise rather than a pure profit-making one, which meant that its aims were to deliver a social impact while being financially sustainable rather than deliver pure profit only. It was quite easy for many of us, at one point, to conclude that we had failed. And we did. However, on closer inspection, we had made a huge impact, just not quite in the way we had expected. We effectively found a niche in one chronic disease area requiring regular treatment three times a week: transporting these patients for their frequent but short treatment cycles was an area that was notoriously difficult to deliver on in a pure profit-making enterprise run by our competitors. Five years on, we now care for, on average, ninety patients at any given time, the majority of whom are very happy with our service, and we are completely independent financially. While this was not quite the financial reward we had intended initially, we had achieved a social reward which, one can argue, is greater. If you ask many of these ninety patients, they certainly would agree.

A conclusion is always based on the vantage point from which you look at a given initiative. I was recently in a photography class, and we were taught this principle about finding and taking good photos – to play with angles and find out how things look. It is amazing how just changing your vantage point can bring out the great photo in your subject, even though the subject is basically the same. So as you come to the end, look at it from as many different angles as you can, the same way as you would looking for a good photograph, before concluding failure. Success is not as obvious as you think, and so much is in the eye of the beholder.

Another key part of the 'So Now What?' chapter goes back to the points made in the 'How?' chapter. You will find that as you progress through the project, opportunities will arise to provide updates and as a final read-out through presentations at key meetings, town halls, board meetings, and other similar events. These official presentations are so important that I will discuss them separately. You can almost look at them as state-of-the-nation addresses by our presidents and prime ministers. At this point, many people

I have worked with make a comment like 'The organisation should plan my career for me', and that is 'The management should know how hard I have worked and how good the project is'. It's a great point, and I accept that, but at the same time, how will they know if you don't tell them? Unfortunately, whether we like it or not, in an MNC, you have to do the telling. It is simply too big and complex an entity for it to happen by itself. You cannot expect the management to know themselves about what you have done with so much competition for their time and attention. As a consequence, a disproportionate amount of credit for a project or perception of its success stems from a very small part of the time used in the project: the presentations. It's a little like a game – the rules are the rules, and these are the rules of the game of an MNC. Just like any other game, if you want to play, you have to follow the rules. After all, we don't argue why rent is highest on Mayfair and Park Lane in Monopoly. It just is, and we go about playing the game using these rules to win.

Given the significant importance of the presentation on the success of the project, it therefore becomes critical to prepare appropriately for it, which means a big investment of time and effort. Many of the teams I work with frown upon this, saying: 'It doesn't bring any value to the project itself'. To which my response is that tremendous value can be created in an indirect round about way, like many things in life. While the presentation doesn't necessarily change the output of the project directly, it can have huge implications elsewhere – for example, access to resources. Recall the example I described earlier around the drug calculator. When it was launched, my challenge to the team was to try to present it like how Steve Jobs would launch the iPhone. Taking that request to heart, rather than just use a laptop and PowerPoint, they worked with IT to enable the whole presentation and use case demos to be driven directly from their iPhone. The way walked around the stage tapping away at their little device would have made Steve proud. This was quite some years ago and at that time, using an iPhone in this way was not common place to say the least. As a consequence, a great deal of testing and rehearsals was required to enable that 10 minutes on stage. However, it was worth it. In my mind, that 10 minute presentation was more impactful than anything else that we did in the early stages of the project. Everything that we created after the drug calculator was only possible thanks to the resources unlocked from this 10 minute vision of the future.

This book isn't specifically a presentation skills book, and it's worth considering to do some research on your own or enrol in a short course around this topic. Nevertheless, there are some key points and stories I want to share. Probably the most useful support (although unusual) that I have received in preparation for a key presentation came from Arthur, one of my ex-managers, as we ended one of the biggest projects I have managed in my career: 'Practice, practice, practice'. He made me write out my entire script, not to read it out but to get my thoughts in order and as a practice aid. We had many dry runs conducted as full dress rehearsals (including wardrobe) where I presented to him as though I were giving the final presentation, and he would critique it. He then asked me to practice at home, to the mirror, and everywhere else I had a chance to – on the flight over, in the hotel room, while sightseeing and eating my meals. My wife honestly thought I had gone insane.

On the big day itself, I was presenting to our entire department globally – a crowd of some four hundred people, the biggest group I had ever spoken in front of at that point in time. I must admit, I had sweaty palms all morning, and just when I thought that there was nothing left to learn, Arthur walked over to me as we prepared to break for lunch. He gave me a pep talk. 'You will present after lunch. Energy will be low with the post-prandial fatigue. So you just need to come up with tremendous energy. Don't forget that. Before you go for lunch, get up on stage, wire yourself up, try the presentation, try the clicker, and just stand up there until you feel you own the room. It's the biggest room you have ever worked, so manage the things that you can. Make sure you know how to use these fiddly things like microphones and laser pointers so it doesn't throw you off.' Like a good soldier, I did all these things. The audiovisual team at the event were impressed to see this level of preparation and gave me a combination of encouraging smiles and some looks of admiration, further boosting my confidence.

It was, quite frankly, the best presentation I have ever made in my life, even till this day, and it led to me getting a promotion not long after. I have taken the exact same approaches with people I have mentored to produce what I can reasonably say were the best presentations many of them had delivered at that point in their careers as well. For a number of them, they also received promotions as a result of some of these best in career presentations. You can count Thena and Wanda from the previous stories among this list. For the managers, this is a time-costly affair, but it is of such importance that it has to be done. The employees amongst you will feel a little like Daniel LaRusso doing the 'wax on, wax off' move to Mr Miyagi in *The Karate Kid*, but persevere, just like the little steps that go into doing the pull-up. It will all come together when you get up on that stage.

Another manager once made two points to me worth highlighting – I'm sorry but I just can't remember who to acknowledge. The first was people have invested a tremendous amount of time to listen to you. Out of respect for that sacrifice, you owe it to them to add value to the time that they have given up. Decide if it is to educate, to entertain, or to inform or something else. Either way, it has to be something. Make up your mind and deliver it. This addresses a lot of the reasons why you should prepare and deliver a presentation impressively.

The next point is about slides. In working on the project, these days, many people will use PowerPoint as a documentation and working tool - a very valid and useful way to work. However, what this also ultimately means is that you will have slides that will be extremely lengthy and wordy. If you work with consultants, this situation is often accentuated given their methodology. These working slides are extremely rich and detailed which if used as is, are too much for a big audience to consume at a read out meeting. This brings me to my manager's second point – your slides are an aid to help you to be more effective, not work as a handicap. The 'less is more' principle is often a great way to achieve this effectiveness. Take a look at the various Apple product launches for inspiration. The simplicity of their slides, paucity of words and simple graphics speak more than a thousand words can. Perhaps it's a bit hard for all industries to be as cool as that, but let's at least try to aspire to something close. This means that you will often need to create a presentation version of your working slides in order to achieve this effect.

During such big presentations, you will be under pressure and, more often than not, will find yourself speaking too quickly. I once attended a presentation skills training where the coach taught us to slow things down when we speak. It allows more time for the brain to process information and results in better speech, less sound fillers, and an easier to understand presentation. Considering that we are often in MNCs presenting to an international audience who are not necessarily speaking the same language as you are as their primary one, slowing down couldn't be more important. The point this trainer made to emphasise matters was that you should feel that you are speaking so preposterously slow, and then only at that point, it is at the right speed. This is because in your heightened state of arousal and nerves with adrenalin pumping, everything will just feel fast. To prove his point, he asked us to speak slowly, record ourselves, and then play back the audio. You will be surprised by just how lovely, eloquent, and smooth you sound despite your perception that it would be like a ridiculous slow motion replay at the finals of your favourite spectator sport.

The other challenge in today's world is that you may have to deliver your presentation virtually on a Zoom or other call. While most of my big presentations were done in real life, there was one major one done virtually. In preparation for this, Arthur, one of my ex-managers, coached me again with some unorthodox methods. They were so effective though that I felt compelled to share more. Apart from the many rehearsals, he made some points about virtual presentations that still hold true today in our post-pandemic world. It's harder to engage virtually, so the level of energy you need to expend is a lot more, and like speaking slowly, it almost has to feel like you are high on drugs for your audience to feel normal levels of energy on the call. The other factor is to get your mindset right. He asked me to dress as though I were delivering the presentation at a hotel to a large group of people. So I remember walking out of the bedroom after dinner in a full suit and tie, drawing the 'I married a lunatic' gaze from my wife. However it's so true that it gets you in the right frame of mind. At a risk of quoting one too many movies, as a Kingsman would say, 'the suit is the armour of the modern knight'. This is a far cry from today's world of wearing your underpants or less on your bottom half in a video call but one which I still believe is worth your consideration. Although it was virtual, I still recall this being the second best presentation in my career.

To wrap up, I want to tell a balancing story and avoid presenting a lopsided view on the need to show off. While it is true that a great deal of effort and planning is needed to communicate, it would not be accurate for me to say that good work is never noticed. There are always people watching in a big MNC, and we have to give them credit as well for being observant. Some years ago, before meeting Magda, we worked with numerous Hoake's disease researchers in the country I was working in at that time. Our aim was to drive up their scientific output as a way of building credibility for the country. The year after we began this initiative, we submitted seven publications to the Asia-Pacific Hoake's disease congress. Little did we know that the rest of the country outside of our group had submitted just four. In a session during the congress, a speaker reviewed the productivity of research in Hoake's disease by different countries and called out these eleven publications from our country. I didn't think much of it at the time but was, of course, enormously proud of the team for the achievement. At the end of the session, Professor Gau, who was the guru of Hoake's disease and founder of its first disease association for the country, came up to us and made the following point: 'Your group is responsible for two-thirds of the country's output this year'. Professor Gau, although a very nice gentleman, was not an individual of many words, but whatever little bit he would offer was genuine and meant in full – good or bad. We had never thought about it in that way, but simply put, it was one of the most subtle yet biggest compliments I have seen bestowed on any team.

While we are grateful for all the Professor Gau's in the world, please still ensure over communication for your special project.

Conclusion

The goal of this book is to help managers earlier in their people management journey and younger single-contributor employees accelerate their career while working in an MNC. While there are many strategies and tactics to do this, the special project in particular delivers in one package all the key components a career acceleration requires – visibility, reputation, network, experience, and learning.

The special project is also the road less travelled because it is often ambiguous and unclear. It lacks the framework and familiarity of other known tactics like doing a course or training. My goal in this book has been to lend some framework to this fuzzy process, starting with 'why' you should do the project, as understanding this is a critical foundation. We then discussed 'which' or 'what' project to do – a careful and deliberate process of ensuring the choosing or creation of a project that will have the highest chance of succeeding. Importantly, we covered how to start this fire going within the employee–manager duet as this is something that cannot be accomplished alone. Once a project has been selected, practical steps should be taken on 'how' to tame such an ambiguous beast, which we reviewed.

Last, we covered the 'Now what?' of finishing the project strong and claiming your prize.

If selected or created well, diligently executed, and communicated strongly, a special project will increase the probability of your career acceleration. While this is philosophical, it is also in this stretch that you will go a long way to better understand the reason of your being. Importantly as well, if enough units of your organisation are working on special projects, it will create an engaging workplace to be in, deliver spectacular results, and create a better world in the sphere that you operate in. These are all significant benefits too big to ignore.

That now leaves me one final point: a call to action. I trust that the stories and thoughts throughout this book have helped demystify the ambiguity of a special project, cutting it down into practical steps to take, and provided inspiration. The rest is now up to you. Without action, this would have just been an academic exercise and light reading. Start having career conversations with your manager or employee. Start looking around for that special project. Start realising your true potential. As the ancient Chinese proverb from Lao Tzu encourages us, 'a journey of a thousand miles begins with a single step'.

Wishing you all great journeys ahead . . .

Acknowledgements

Cover Recognitions

Cover Photography: Wilson Tan, long-time collaborator and friend

Author Portrait: Wilson Tan, long-time collaborator and friend

CPSIA information can be obtained
at www.ICGtesting.com
Printed in the USA
LVHW100506130422
716029LV00002B/13

9 781543 768718